CQ Press's Guide to the 2010 Midterm Elections

Gregory Giroux

CQ PRESS

A Division of SAGE
Washington, D.C.

CQ Press
2300 N Street, NW, Suite 800
Washington, DC 20037

Phone: 202-729-1900; toll-free, 1-866-4CQ-PRESS (1-866-427-7737)

Web: www.cqpress.com

Copyright © 2010 by CQ Press, a division of SAGE. CQ Press is a registered trademark of Congressional Quarterly Inc.

All rights reserved. No part of this publication may be reproduced or transmitted in any form or by any means, electronic or mechanical, including photocopy, recording, or any information storage and retrieval system, without permission in writing from the publisher.

Cover design: Paula Goldstein
Composition: C&M Digitals (P) Ltd.
Photo credits:
AP Images: 10, 13, 17, 34 (top), 45 (both)
Corbis: 23, 27
Courtesy of the Office of Congressman Chris Van Hollen: 14 (top)
Courtesy of the Office of Congressman Pete Sessions: 14 (bottom)
Courtesy of the Office of Senator Bob Menendez: 15 (bottom)
Courtesy of the Office of Senator John Cornyn: 15 (top)
Courtesy of the Office of Tim Kaine: 16
Getty Images: 1, 8, 11, 25, 34 (center), 44
Reuters: 12, 34 (bottom)
Young Guns screenshot/www.gopyoungguns.com: 19

∞ The paper used in this publication exceeds the requirements of the American National Standard for Information Sciences—Permanence of Paper for Printed Library Materials, ANSI Z39.48–1992.

Printed and bound in the United States of America

14 13 12 11 10   1 2 3 4 5

ISBN 978-1-60871-683-8

Contents

2010 Midterm Elections: A Lasting Imprint on Society	1
Why 2010 Will Not Be a Repeat of 1994	3
Lessons from Off-Year and Special Elections	6
Democrats with the Edge in New York	7
Republican Governors in Virginia and New Jersey	9
A Surprise Upset in Massachusetts	10
Democrats Hold On in Pennsylvania	12
Republicans Take Hawaii with Split Democrat Vote	18
Role of the Party Committees	18
Role of Outside Groups	20
Issues in the 2010 Election	24
The Economy	24
Health Care Reform	26
Other Issues	26
Key Senate Races	28
Democratic-Held States	28
Republican-Held States	35
Key House Races	37
Key Gubernatorial Races	39
Democratic-Held Seats	39
Republican-Held Seats	42
Dress Rehearsal for 2012	44
Notes	46

OUTLINE:

2010 Midterm Elections: A Lasting Imprint on Society

Why 2010 Will Not Be a Repeat of 1994

Lessons from Off-Year and Special Elections

Role of the Party Committees

Role of Outside Groups

Issues in the 2010 Election

Key Senate Races

Key House Races

Key Gubernatorial Races

Dress Rehearsal for 2012

Many Democrats in Congress will be fighting hard to keep their jobs in the 2010 midterm elections, including Senate majority leader Harry Reid of Nevada, shown campaigning in Fernley, Nevada, on April 6, 2010. Reid, who is seeking a fifth six-year term, is trying to avoid becoming the first Senate majority leader to lose a re-election bid in nearly six decades.

2010 Midterm Elections: A Lasting Imprint on Society

As a rule, midterm elections do not attract as much attention or coverage as presidential elections. Voter turnout rates for midterm elections are much lower than for presidential elections—tens of millions of Americans who vote for president just don't vote in congressional elections.

The 2010 midterm elections, however, will leave a lasting imprint on society and will be consequential for many reasons. First and foremost, all 435 U.S. House seats and 36 Senate seats will be at stake, and the results will determine the partisan composition of the 112th Congress that will convene in January 2011. Large Republican gains, including the capture of one or both chambers by the Grand Old Party

(GOP), would complicate the policy agenda of President Barack Obama in the second half of his first term, when he will be positioning himself for re-election in 2012.

Republicans are expected to make gains in both the House and the Senate this November, if only because history says they will. In most midterm elections the party in control of the White House loses ground in Congress, in part because the opposition party generally has more energy and enthusiasm than the defending party. Also in keeping with historical trends, President Obama's approval rating is not as strong now as it was early in his presidency.

Still, it will be very difficult for the Republicans to overturn the Democratic majorities in the House and the Senate. The Republicans need a net gain of 39 seats to reach a majority of 218, something they have done only once in the past four decades—in the watershed 1994 elections in which they netted 54 seats. Some Republicans have drawn comparisons between 2010 and 1994, but it is an uneven one. Among the factors hampering the Republican campaign are a dearth of retirements in Democratic ranks and a big fund-raising disadvantage.

In the Senate, the Republicans' odds of winning a majority are even longer: the Democrats hold fifty-nine of the one hundred seats, requiring the GOP to make a net gain of ten seats. That will be exceptionally difficult to accomplish, given that the Democrats are the defending party in eighteen Senate races and the Republicans are the defending party in eighteen others. Yet it seemed likely in the spring of 2010 that the GOP would net at least five Senate seats, which would put the party in striking distance of securing a majority in 2012, when Democrats will be the defending party in more than half of the Senate races that will be at stake.

TABLE 1
Losses by the President's Party in Midterm Elections since World War II

Year	White House Party	House Result	Senate Result
1946	D	−55	−12
1950	D	−29	−6
1954	R	−18	−1
1958	R	−47	−13
1962	D	−5	3
1966	D	−47	−4
1970	R	−12	3
1974	R	−48	−5
1978	D	−15	−3
1982	R	−26	1
1986	R	−5	−8
1990	R	−7	−1
1994	D	−54	−10
1998	D	4	0
2002	R	8	2
2006	R	−30	−6

Source: Howard W. Stanley and Richard G. Niemi, *Vital Statistics on American Politics, 2009–2010* (Washington, D.C.: CQ Press, 2009).

Moreover, the 2010 midterm elections will have significant implications for the process of congressional redistricting that will ensue in early 2011, after the census determines how many House districts each of the fifty states is entitled to receive. In most states the congressional lines are redrawn by partisan legislators who will be trying to give their parties a greater political advantage. To that end, map-making technology is now so advanced that legislators can draw new lines with surgical precision.

Incumbents and candidates in both parties are confronting an electorate that is angry and frustrated with the direction of the country, the sluggish pace of the economy, and what they see as the inability of Congress to solve major problems. There were signs in early 2010 that incumbents generally and Democratic officeholders in particular could have a challenging year.

Why 2010 Will Not Be a Repeat of 1994

When examining possible outcomes of the 2010 midterm elections, it is necessary to keep in mind that there are important differences between 2010 and 1994. One is that the Republican Party has a poorer image in 2010, less than four years removed from majority status, than in 1994, when it hadn't won a House majority in forty years.

"No one could really fathom or relate to what a Republican takeover would mean, except change. In 2010, many voters still have a bitter aftertaste from GOP rule (which only ended in 2006) and will be more reluctant to vote for a Republican as an automatic alternative," former Virginia Republican representative Thomas M. Davis III, a former chair of the National Republican Congressional Committee (NRCC), wrote in November 2009.[1]

A Gallup poll conducted in late May 2010 found that the Republican Party had a favorable rating of just 36 percent, not far above the 31 percent that was the lowest rating Republicans had received since the polling organization began measuring such statistics in 1992.[2]

Second, not many House Democrats are retiring or seeking other office. (Such "open" districts often are more difficult for the defending party to win than those in which well-funded and well-known incumbents are seeking re-election.) Just eighteen House Democrats are leaving their seats open this year, compared to thirty-one in 1994. Republicans won twenty-two of those thirty-one districts.

A third major difference between the two election years is that the Democrats are better prepared for a Republican upswing than they were in 1994, when the GOP "wave" developed late in the election year.

This isn't to say that the Republicans can't make substantial gains. The Democratic Party's image also has lost some of its luster in recent years. In the May 2010 Gallup poll, the party's 43 percent favorable rating was just ahead of the record-low 41 percent favorable rating that Gallup measured in March 2010.

TIMELINE

MIDTERM ELECTIONS IN HISTORICAL CONTEXT

To understand the importance of midterm elections—and why Republicans are expected to make gains in this year's balloting—it is instructive to look at midterm election history. Here's a look at the sixteen midterm elections since the end of World War II; in all but two instances—1998 and 2002—the party in control of the White House lost ground in the House of Representatives.

1946 — Harry S. Truman had been president for barely eighteen months when Republicans made huge gains in the November 1946 midterm elections, gaining majorities in both chambers.
"Having assumed the presidency in April 1945 after the death of Franklin D. Roosevelt, Truman had large shoes to fill," according to the political scientist Andrew E. Busch. "Inflation was rising, labor unrest concerned many, most wartime economic controls remained in place, and tensions with Joseph Stalin were already escalating. After fourteen years of unified Democratic control of government, voters were ready for a change."[3]
Democrats also were hurt by Truman's dismissal of commerce secretary and former vice president Henry Wallace in September, as well as by a seven-week national meat shortage just before the election. Republican slogans included "Had enough?" and "It's time for a change."

1950 — The euphoria for Democrats following Truman's come-from-behind re-election victory in 1948 had dissipated by the midterm election year. Republicans sharply criticized the administration on issues such as inflation, the conflict in Korea, and communism, and they made strong gains in the House and Senate.

1954 — Two years after Republican Dwight D. Eisenhower won a landslide election that ushered in GOP majorities in the House and Senate, the Democrats made a comeback and won back control of both chambers. Eisenhower injected himself into the congressional elections, telling voters that Congress had passed most of his legislative proposals. The implication was that more would get done in government if the same party held both Congress and the executive office. In a televised appearance one month before the election, he charged that a Democratic congressional victory would start "a cold war of partisan politics between the Congress and the Executive Branch," which would block "the great work" his administration had "begun so well."[4] Yet Eisenhower's entreaties weren't enough to stem the Democratic upswing.

1958 — An economic recession that took hold in the sixth year of Eisenhower's administration was a major reason why Democrats made large gains in the midterm elections. Republicans also antagonized organized labor by pushing for "right to work" laws in a number of states.
Democrats won a whopping thirteen Senate seats from Republican control and also won both Senate seats in Alaska as it prepared to achieve statehood in January 1959.
The only member of this banner Democratic class who continues to serve today is West Virginia senator Robert C. Byrd, who became the longest-serving senator in history in 2006 and the longest-serving member of Congress in history in 2009.

1962 — Two years into John F. Kennedy's presidency, Democrats only sustained minor losses. One reason: the public rallied around Kennedy following his handling of the Cuban missile crisis. As *Congressional Quarterly* reported at the time, "Observers said that the Cuban crisis, developing only a few days before the elections, might have solidified support behind the President, cancelled out a central Republican campaign issue, and thus minimized Republican gains that might otherwise have occurred."[5]

1966 — The Democrats had made substantial gains in Congress in 1964, when President Lyndon B. Johnson was elected in a landslide. The thorough rout of the GOP—coupled with the Democrats' enactment of a raft of social policy legislation in 1965 (including Medicare)—made it unlikely that the Republicans would bounce back so quickly.

4 CQ Press's Guide to the 2010 Midterm Elections

But they did. The escalation of the Vietnam War became unpopular with the public, and Johnson's approval ratings suffered.

The Republicans scored a net gain of forty-seven House seats and four Senate seats, and the new Republican governors included Ronald Reagan in California.

As political analyst Rhodes Cook noted about the 1966 elections, "For the first time, Republicans showed signs of becoming a truly national party by expanding the beachheads the party had already made across the South. The GOP inroads made clear that the region was no longer solidly Democratic, but one that could embrace conservative Republicanism."

President Richard M. Nixon's Republican Party sustained modest losses in House elections in which Nixon made an unprecedented effort to campaign for the party's candidates. In the weeks preceding the election, he stumped for candidates in twenty-three states and Vice President Spiro Agnew campaigned in twenty-nine states.[6] Republicans actually made a three-seat gain in the Senate, mainly because the Democrats were defending more than twice as many seats as the Republicans that year.

1970

Nixon's resignation in the Watergate scandal less than three months before the November midterm elections had catastrophic consequences for Republicans. The Democrats made a net gain of forty-eight seats in the House, giving the party more than two-thirds of the overall House seats. The Democrats also gained five seats in the Senate races.

1974

The midpoint of President Jimmy Carter's term was pretty quiet by historical standards. The Democrats lost fifteen seats in the House and three seats in the Senate but still retained large majorities in both chambers.

1978

A deep recession put Republicans on the defensive two years after Ronald Reagan's landslide election as president had ushered in a GOP Senate majority and also spurred big gains in the House. Democrats also outperformed Republicans in the redistricting process. With a twenty-six-seat gain, Democrats erased most of the thirty-three-seat gain the Republicans had made in 1980. Republicans managed to hold their own in the Senate though.

1982

The Senate majority the Republicans won in the 1980 Reagan landslide was reversed by the Democrats, who made a net gain of eight seats to take a 55–45 majority. Many GOP freshmen brought in on Reagan's coattails showed weakness in a less favorable political environment and against determined Democratic opposition. A depressed farm economy helped Democrats unseat Republicans in North Dakota and South Dakota. In the House elections the Republicans lost a modest five seats.

1986

A budget agreement between President George H.W. Bush and the Democratic-run Congress "prevented the election from becoming a referendum on economic policy," according to CQ Press's *Guide to U.S. Elections*. "Divisive issues such as taxes and abortion played out inconsistently across party and state lines. Even the growing prospects for war with Iraq failed to stir a wide-ranging debate over U.S. policy in the Persian Gulf."[7]

Many incumbents saw their re-election percentages reduced but few lost. Republicans suffered a modest loss of seven seats in the House and one in the Senate.

1990

Republicans made huge gains in the first midterm of President Bill Clinton's tenure, gaining control of the House for the first time in forty years and the Senate for the first time in fourteen years. The GOP proposed a ten-point "Contract With America"—a promise to make Congress more accountable to the public—and ran against Clinton's deficit-reduction package on the grounds that it included excessive and unnecessary tax hikes. But the Democrats also suffered from self-inflicted wounds, including the party's humiliating failure to pass a crime bill three months before the election.

The GOP's net gain of fifty-four House seats was punctuated by the defeat of some senior Democrats, including Speaker Tom Foley of Washington State, Dan Rostenkowski of Illinois, Jack Brooks of Texas, and Neal Smith of Iowa.

1994

1998 — The Republicans made a net gain of nine seats in the Senate during the election cycle, adding a tenth two days after the election, when conservative Democratic senator Richard Shelby announced he was switching parties.

In a departure from historical norms, Democrats actually made a net gain of four House seats at the midpoint of President Clinton's second term, the first time since 1934 that the White House's party made gains in a midterm election. Clinton, a student of political history, noted that it also was the first time since 1822 that the president's party made seat gains in the sixth year of an administration.

So how it did happen, especially in light of so many political pundits suggesting that the disclosure in January of President Clinton's relations with Monica Lewinsky would cause Democratic voters to stay home? In reality, it appeared to have the opposite effect, as some voters felt that the Republicans overreached in their efforts to impeach the president. It also helped Democrats that the economy was strong and the nation was at peace.

There was no change in the partisan composition of the Senate, which remained at fifty-five Republicans and forty-five Democrats.

2002 — Republicans gained seats in the House and Senate at the midpoint of President Bush's first term in large part because of a favorable political environment that prevailed for Bush and Republicans in the aftermath of the September 11, 2001, terrorist attacks. The president campaigned in fifteen states in the final week of the campaign.

Republicans also had the upper hand in the redistricting process, controlling the line-drawing process in populous states like Michigan and Pennsylvania. Republicans also won three of the four races in which a Republican incumbent was pitted against a Democratic incumbent.

The net result on Election Day was that the Republicans had eight more House seats than they did at the beginning of the Congress.

In the Senate, the Republicans made a net gain of two seats, which was just enough to overturn the one-seat majority Democrats had gained after GOP senator James Jeffords announced in May 2001 that he was leaving the Republican Party to become a Democratic-leaning independent.

A key win came in Minnesota, where Republican Norm Coleman narrowly beat Democratic former vice president Walter Mondale, who became his party's candidate following the death of Democratic senator Paul Wellstone in a plane crash less than two weeks before the election.

2006 — What narrow mandate President George W. Bush earned in his close 2004 re-election campaign quickly dissipated. The war in Iraq, which had reached its fourth year as 2006 began, became more

"Even though Democrats currently maintain higher favorable ratings than Republicans, the Republicans still seem poised for a strong showing in the fall midterm elections," Gallup pollsters reported. "Registered voter preferences in Gallup's generic ballot are divided equally between the parties, which would generally indicate a stronger Republican year given the party's usual advantage in voter turnout."[8]

Lessons from Off-Year and Special Elections

Clues into how the midterm political winds may be blowing can be gleaned by the results of special elections that are sometimes held to fill unexpected vacancies caused by death or resignation. Because these elections are held months before the unpopular, and the aftermath of Hurricane Katrina in the summer of 2005 exposed glaring shortcomings in how the federal government handled the crisis. A string of corruption scandals involving Republican members of Congress also battered the party's image. Democratic organizations, particularly the Democratic Congressional Campaign Committee (DCCC) under Illinois representative Rahm Emanuel and the Democratic Senatorial Campaign Committee (DSCC) under New York senator Charles E. Schumer, raised copious amounts of campaign cash to stay competitive with the majority-party Republicans.

The Democrats made a net gain of thirty House seats, unseating twenty-two Republican incumbents and winning eight districts that Republican incumbents had left open upon retiring or seeking another office. The Democrats didn't lose a single race in which they were the defending party.

In the Senate elections, a six-seat Democratic gain was just enough for the party to turn a 55–45 Republican majority into a 51–49 Democratic edge.

2010?

That brings us to 2010. As history shows, the White House's party much more often than not loses ground in Congress in midterm elections.

This year's elections certainly will follow the general rule. The question is not whether or not Republicans will make seat gains—even Democratic strategists have acknowledged that will likely occur—but what the size of those gains will be.

Will 2010 be more like 1962, when Democrats lost few seats two years into President Kennedy's term? Or will it resemble 1994, when Republicans made huge gains in both the House and Senate at the midpoint of President Clinton's first term? Or will the Democratic losses be somewhere in between?

Republican strategists are hopeful for another 1994. They point to the low approval ratings of Congress and to much of the voting public's opposition to a health care overhaul that Obama signed into law in March 2010. On the Republican side, candidate recruitment is strong, and the party is contesting Democratic-held districts where the GOP hasn't seriously competed in years, if not decades.

A case in point is Missouri's west central 4th district, where Democratic representative Ike Skelton has held his office since 1977. He chairs the House Armed Services Committee. Though the district has strong conservative leanings—John McCain won 61 percent of the district vote in the 2008 presidential election—Skelton has cultivated an image as a centrist-to-conservative Democrat and dominated all of his re-election campaigns. Republicans scarcely fielded serious challengers against Skelton—until 2010, when a state senator and a former state House member were among the nine challengers vying to oppose the congressman.

national balloting, they often attract outsized attention as potential barometers of voters' feelings.

Democrats with the Edge in New York

The first major special election of the 2010 campaign cycle occurred March 31, 2009, in New York's 20th district, a collection of upstate suburban and rural areas near Albany that Democratic representative Kirsten E. Gillibrand had given up to accept an appointment to the U.S. Senate. New York's 20th is a historically Republican but politically competitive district, having voted for Republican George W. Bush in his 2004 re-election and then for Democrat Barack Obama in 2008. Gillibrand had won the seat in 2006, unseating a four-term Republican.

Rep. Bill Owens (D-N.Y.) shakes hands with House Speaker Nancy Pelosi (D-Calif.) during a mock swearing-in on November 6, 2009, three days after he won a special election in a historically Republican district in upstate New York. Owens benefited from a split in the Republican Party and will be competitively challenged in the 2010 election.

Republicans had the early edge in the race, in part because of a seeming disparity in the quality of the candidates the two parties fielded to run in the special election. The GOP candidate was Jim Tedisco, a veteran legislator and the minority leader of the New York Assembly at the time of the election. The Democrats selected Scott Murphy, a businessman and investor who had never run for political office.

Tedisco led early in the polls, but Murphy turned out to be a good candidate. He struck a moderate tone and campaigned on a platform of job creation and support for President Obama's economic agenda, including an economic stimulus plan that Obama signed into law in mid-February. Murphy's message resonated in the district—which was economically struggling, like much of New York—and he edged Tedisco by a few hundred votes to keep the district in Democratic hands and deprive Republicans of a momentum-building victory.

Seven months later, another upstate New York district held a special election—the 23rd district of Republican representative John McHugh, who resigned to become Obama's Army secretary. McHugh's district leaned Republican, and he had won all of his re-election campaigns easily, but a nasty split in the GOP allowed little-known Democratic lawyer Bill Owens to steal the victory in the November 3, 2009, balloting.

Unlike in most states, in New York a party nominee in a special election is chosen by a small committee of party officials and not by a broad swath of voters in a primary election. The GOP officials in New York's 23rd chose Dede Scozzafava, a member of the state Assembly.

Scozzafava's left-leaning views on social issues were anathema to many conservatives in the district, however, and they sided with Doug Hoffman, an accountant who ran as the nominee of the Conservative Party, which has ballot access in New York. Hoffman overtook Scozzafava in the polls, and pressure from the right wing compelled her to withdraw from the race three days before the balloting. Scozzafava endorsed Owens, who took 50 percent of the vote to 45 percent for Hoffman, who is seeking a rematch this year.

Republicans blamed the candidate selection process for their loss. Republican National Committee (RNC) chair Michael Steele described New York's 23rd district as "a special election with a very messed-up process."

"This is an example of what happens when a small group of individuals select the nominee without the opportunity for the primary voter, Republican voter, to express who they want to represent them in the general election," he said.[9]

Democrats were ecstatic at capturing a district that had been in Republican hands for decades. Party officials suggested that the result showed that Republican moderates are getting elbowed out of the party.

"I think what's happening in the Republican Party is you're seeing no moderates need apply. The moderates, the centrists, that core part of what used to be the Republican Party is basically getting forced out by extremist candidates," said Democratic National Committee (DNC) chair Tim Kaine.[10]

Republican Governors in Virginia and New Jersey

But on the same day that Owens won in upstate New York, the Republican Party scored meaningful and symbolic victories in governor's races in Virginia and New Jersey, which elect their chief executives in the year following a presidential election.

In Virginia, Republican state attorney general Bob McDonnell trounced Democratic state senator Creigh Deeds, 59 percent to 41 percent, to succeed Kaine as governor. McDonnell attacked Deeds for backing several tax hikes in the state legislature, and while he didn't frequently attack Obama, McDonnell did nationalize the Virginia race by running as an opponent of a "cap and trade" climate change bill that he said would be harmful to the state's economy.

In New Jersey, Republican Chris Christie, a former federal prosecutor, unseated Democratic governor Jon Corzine, 49 percent to 45 percent, and ended eight years of Democratic control of the governor's office. Christie led the race from start to finish, aided by Corzine's poor approval ratings over his handling of the state's flagging economy.

Republicans seized on the results in Virginia and New Jersey as repudiation of the economic policies of the Obama administration and Democratic leaders.

"What's important, I think, to take out of these elections is that voters in both states were very concerned about the direction on the economy, and rejected out of hand the economic policies being pursued by the White House and Speaker [Nancy] Pelosi," Rep. Eric Cantor (R-Va.), the House minority whip, said the day after the election.[11]

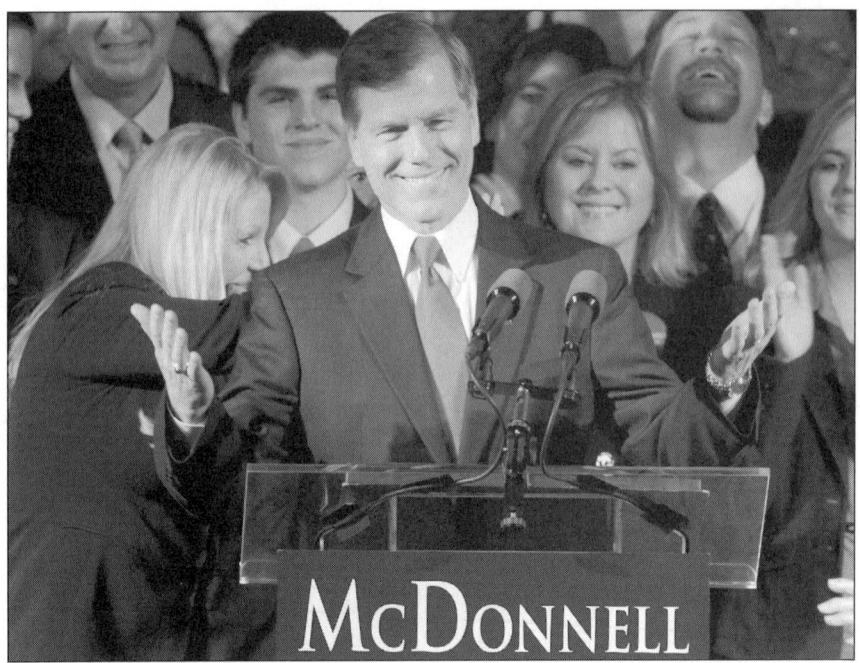

Republicans Bob McDonnell of Virginia (left) and Chris Christie of New Jersey (right) acknowledge supporters after claiming victories in key gubernatorial races on November 3, 2009. Republicans claimed the twin wins would give their party momentum heading into the midterm elections, though

Democrats generally downplayed the results in Virginia and New Jersey as in keeping with historical norms of the opposition party winning governorships in off-year elections. The White House's party last won the New Jersey governorship in 1985 and the Virginia governorship in 1973.

"So there is a little bit of a trend at work here, where we felt like we were running uphill in both races because of the economy and this historic trend," Kaine said on MSNBC the day after the election.

A Surprise Upset in Massachusetts

At the time of the Republican victories in Virginia and New Jersey and the Democratic wins in New York, almost no one expected that a special Senate election in Massachusetts in January 2010 would be competitive.

Democratic senator Edward M. Kennedy, who died in August 2009 after a battle with brain cancer, had dominated his re-election campaigns, and Massachusetts's Democratic proclivities were evident also in giving nearly 62 percent of the vote to Barack Obama in 2008, his eighth-best performance in the fifty states.[12]

Democrats downplayed the results as having limited predictive value and being consistent with a historical trend of the White House's party losing the Virginia and New Jersey governorships one year after the presidential election.

But state senator Scott Brown, the Republican nominee, ran a strong campaign in which he said that the Senate seat "belongs to the people" of Massachusetts and not to one person or political party.

He also emphasized national security, an issue that was on voters' minds after Nigerian citizen Umar Farouk Abdulmutallab attempted to detonate plastic explosives while on board a flight from Amsterdam to Michigan on Christmas Day 2009.

"His message was what resonated with voters. He talked about terror. He talked about taxes. He talked about spending. He talked about jobs. And those are all things that are on everyone's minds right now," said Jennifer Nasour, chair of the Massachusetts Republican Party.[13]

Brown also was helped by a lackluster campaign from Democratic nominee Martha Coakley, the state attorney general who seemed to take a victory for granted and who didn't campaign as vigorously as Brown. She made several missteps, including scoffing at shaking hands with voters outside Boston's venerable Fenway Park. Not even a last-minute campaign visit from President Obama could save Coakley, who lost to Brown 52 percent to 47 percent. Brown became the first Republican to win a Senate election in Massachusetts since Edward Brooke was re-elected in 1972.

Scott Brown's election in January 2010 to a Senate seat in Massachusetts was an early and clear sign of voter disgust at the political status quo. An obscure but telegenic Republican in the nation's most reliably Democratic state, Brown won the seat of late Democratic senator Edward M. Kennedy in part by tapping into voters' disenchantment with Washington, D.C. The Democratic nominee, state attorney general Martha Coakley, ran a campaign that often seemed uninspired and presumptive of victory.

Democratic officials described the Massachusetts election as a wake-up call for their party and a warning that no one should take an election for granted in such a volatile election year. These officials also acknowledged that the election reflected the deep anxieties many voters have about the economy.

"I think the main thing that we saw in Massachusetts was the same sense of concern on the part of middle-class folks about the economic situation, about their wages being stagnant, about jobs being lost, about their economic security that's been in jeopardy," said David Axelrod, a senior adviser to President Obama.[14]

Democrats Hold On in Pennsylvania

The next special election to garner substantial national attention came in Pennsylvania's 12th district, a politically competitive swath in the southwestern part of the state, in the spring of 2010. Democratic representative John P. Murtha had dominated the district during a House career that spanned nearly four decades and was punctuated by his acquisition of vast sums of federal monies for his district.

Democrat Mark Critz celebrates after winning a nationally significant special election in Pennsylvania's 12th district on May 18, 2010, succeeding his former boss, the late Democratic representative John Murtha. Republicans had targeted the district, but Critz won by a surprisingly large margin of eight percentage points.

Murtha's death in February 2010 necessitated a May special election to replace him. A highly competitive race was anticipated in a district that has the distinction of being the only congressional district in the nation to back John McCain for president in 2008 four years after voting for John Kerry, the 2004 Democratic presidential nominee.

The nominees in the special election were determined by committees of local party officials. The Democrats chose Mark Critz, Murtha's former district director, and the Republicans went with Tim Burns, a businessman.

One poll pegged Obama's approval rating in Pennsylvania's 12th district at just 35 percent, and so Republicans worked to nationalize the race around an opposition to the policies of the president and Democratic leaders. Burns frequently invoked House Speaker Nancy Pelosi, a California liberal.

Critz ran as a moderate-to-conservative Democrat not unlike Murtha. He opposed abortion, gun control, and a "cap and trade" climate change bill, and said he had problems with the new health care law—but also resisted calls by Burns and other Republicans to repeal it. He focused on local economic development and deflected the GOP focus on national politics by saying he was more concerned about Washington County, Pennsylvania, than about Washington, D.C.

Lessons from Off-Year and Special Elections

Chris Van Hollen (D-Md.)
Chair, Democratic Congressional Campaign Committee (DCCC)

Van Hollen, who is leading the House Democrats' campaign organization for the second consecutive election cycle, has a very different demeanor and reputation from his predecessor in the job.

Whereas Rahm Emanuel, who led Democrats to a majority in the 2006 election and later became President Obama's chief of staff, was well known for his ruthlessness and profanity-laced intensity, Van Hollen has a calm, nice-guy demeanor.

As Rep. Debbie Wasserman (D-Fla.) put it, "Rahm is Type A on steroids, and Chris is a milkshake. A really good milkshake, but a milkshake—somebody who is even keeled and very steady."[15]

Beneath the friendly exterior, though, lies a reservoir of political skill and ambition. A graduate of Swarthmore College who later took a public policy degree from Harvard University and a law degree from Georgetown University, Van Hollen won his first election in 1990, securing a seat in the Maryland House of Delegates at age thirty-one.

Van Hollen's political skills have drawn praise even from adversaries.

"There's no question he's smart, he's articulate, he's got a belief structure that he holds quite sincerely. . . . I have a very healthy respect for his political skills and his personal integrity and dedication to his job," said Rep. Tom Cole (R-Okla.), who headed the National Republican Congressional Committee during the 2008 cycle.[16]

Aided by the successful presidential campaign of Barack Obama, Van Hollen guided the DCCC to a net gain of two dozen House seats in the 2008 election cycle—including victories in three key special elections in the spring.

Van Hollen planned to step down from the DCCC chair after the 2008 election but was encouraged to continue by Speaker Nancy Pelosi, who gave him added policy responsibilities as one of her top lieutenants. He also is a key House liaison to the Obama White House.

Van Hollen has frequently been mentioned as a candidate for the Senate, though he declined to run in 2006 for the seat of retiring Democratic senator Paul Sarbanes. The Speakership could also be in his sights in the not-too-distant future: just fifty-one years old in 2010, Van Hollen is about twenty years younger than each of the top three ranking House Democratic leaders.

Pete Sessions (R-Texas)
Chair, National Republican Congressional Committee (NRCC)

Sessions, who was first elected in 1996 to represent part of Dallas and some of its suburbs, has an easygoing manner that belies deep political ambition.

He made it to Congress on his third try, first losing the Republican nomination for a vacant House seat in 1991 and then falling to Democratic representative John Bryant in an adjacent district three years later. After that second loss, Sessions worked as vice president for public policy at the National Center for Policy Analysis, a conservative think tank in Dallas.

In 1996, when Bryant left his seat open to run for the Senate, Sessions was narrowly elected. Early in his tenure he was named chair of the Results Caucus, a now-defunct group that promoted ways to streamline government.

Sessions has usually won his re-election campaigns with ease. One exception was in 2004, when a new redistricting plan drawn up by Texas Republican legislators paired Sessions with veteran Democratic representative Martin Frost in a district that favored Sessions.

Sessions eyed the NRCC chair after Republicans lost their House majority in the 2006 elections. He placed second in a three-way race for the position ultimately won by Oklahoma representative Tom Cole. Sessions won the job after Republicans sustained more losses after the 2008 elections.

John Cornyn (R-Texas)
Chair, National Republican Senatorial Committee (NRSC)

For most of his Senate career, Cornyn was known as a supporter of the priorities of President George W. Bush, a fellow Texan. This supporting role included helping to shepherd Bush's judicial nominees to confirmation.

As the NRSC chair, Cornyn has assumed a higher profile as a leading Republican spokesperson and strategist who is helping lead the opposition against President Obama and the Democrats' Senate majority.

Upon taking the NRSC chair, Cornyn vowed that the organization would be more competitive in fund-raising with the Democratic Senatorial Campaign Committee, which had raised more than $60 million more than the NRSC in the 2007–2008 campaign cycle.

Through the first sixteen months of the 2009–2010 election cycle, the NRSC raised $60.4 million, well ahead of its pace in the previous cycle and nearly at parity with the DSCC, which raised $61.9 million.

Cornyn majored in journalism and earned a real estate license but later switched to the legal profession. In 1984, when Democrats were still the dominant party in Texas politics, Cornyn ran for a state district court seat and won. He served six years and was elected in 1990 to the Texas Supreme Court. In 1998 he was elected state attorney general, and four years later he was the Republicans' consensus pick for the U.S. Senate seat of retiring Republican senator Phil Gramm. He won the election by twelve percentage points and captured a second term in 2008 by the same margin.

Robert Menendez (D-N.J.)
Chair, Democratic Senatorial Campaign Committee (DSCC)

Ambitious and aggressive, Menendez caught the political bug at a young age and is now one of the Democratic Party's top political strategists.

Menendez has big shoes to fill as the successor to Sen. Charles E. Schumer. For one, Menendez doesn't have the enormous fund-raising clout of Schumer, long one of Congress's biggest money-raisers. In addition, he's running the Democratic Senate campaign at a time when his party is on the defensive after gaining fourteen Senate seats over the previous two election cycles.

Menendez currently is the only Hispanic senator, and he's hoping to boost the voter participation of Latino voters in the 2010 election. "In this particular election cycle, there are a series of states in which the Hispanic community will play a very significant role," he said in April 2009.[17]

He won his first office in 1974, when he was elected to the school board at age twenty as a college undergraduate. He was elected mayor of Union City in 1986 and to the state Assembly in 1987. He served briefly in the state Senate in the early 1990s and won an open U.S. House seat in 1992. He served for about thirteen years, reaching the number three position in the Democratic leadership as the party's caucus chair. He was appointed to the Senate in early 2006 by the seat's previous holder, Jon Corzine, who had been elected governor. Menendez was elected to a full six-year term in November 2006.

"Is he aggressive? Yeah," Corzine said of Menendez in 2006. "But I believe in competency and people who get things done, and Bob is one of those people."[18]

Tim Kaine (D-Va.)
Chair, Democratic National Committee (DNC)

It was not a surprise when President Obama asked Kaine to chair the DNC, the umbrella political organization that works to elect as many Democrats as possible at all levels of office.

After all, Kaine had been an early backer of Obama's quest for the presidency at a time when the preponderance of Democratic opinion was in the corner of New York senator Hillary Rodham Clinton. Obama's landslide victory over Clinton in the February 2008 Virginia Democratic primary made Kaine look prescient.

Obama seriously considered Kaine to be his vice-presidential running mate, but ultimately went with Delaware senator Joseph R. Biden Jr.

Kaine was born in 1958 in Minnesota and grew up in the Kansas City area. During a one-year break in his studies at Harvard Law School, Kaine served as a Catholic missionary in Honduras.

Polls showed a close race, but the final result gave Critz a surprisingly strong victory of 53 percent to 45 percent.

Republicans said they were disappointed by the result, which they attributed in part to the special election being held on the same day as the regular statewide primary election in which Sen. Arlen Specter and Rep. Joe Sestak were engaged in a competitive race that boosted Democratic turnout.

He was elected mayor of Richmond in 1998 and then narrowly won the lieutenant governorship in 2001, when Democrat Mark Warner was elected governor. With Warner unable to run in 2005 for a second consecutive term under Virginia's strict term-limits law, Kaine won the election to succeed him. He finished out his term as governor in early 2010 and was succeeded by Republican Bob McDonnell.

Michael Steele (R-Md.)
Chair, Republican National Committee (RNC)

Steele had hoped to be a U.S. senator from Maryland by now, though his career trajectory has brought him to the helm of the RNC as its first black chair.

Steele originally planned to become a Catholic priest but left the seminary to pursue a career in law. He also was active in Republican politics as chair of the party in Prince George's County, Maryland, just outside Washington, D.C., and he became chair of that state's Republican Party in 2000.

Two years later Rep. Robert L. Ehrlich Jr., the Republicans' candidate for governor, tapped Steele to be his lieutenant governor running mate on a ticket that was successful in the fall. Steele chose not to seek re-election with Ehrlich in 2006 and instead sought an open U.S. Senate seat, though he lost the election to Democrat Ben Cardin.

After that loss, Steele angled for the RNC chair, but the post went to Florida senator Mel Martinez. Steele sought the post again when it opened up after Barack Obama's election as president, and he won the election in January 2009 on the fifth ballot.

Steele's tenure has been rocky at times. In March 2009, he raised eyebrows—and the ire of conservative activists—when he said that popular conservative broadcaster Rush Limbaugh's "whole thing is entertainment. Yes, it is incendiary. Yes, it is ugly."[19] Also that month, Steele came under fire for telling *GQ* magazine that abortion is "absolutely . . . an individual choice," a position that puts him at odds with most members of his party.

Steele's gaffes sparked some speculation that he might be replaced as RNC chair before the end of the election cycle. But that seemed highly unlikely, in part because such an action requires a two-thirds vote.[20]

Democrats praised Critz's campaign, particularly his familiarity with the district and his emphasis on boosting economic development. They also dismissed as ineffective the Republicans' strategy to link Democratic candidates to Speaker Nancy Pelosi of California.

"The idea they will win by demagoguing Pelosi has been proven a losing strategy," current DCCC chair Chris Van Hollen said shortly after Critz's victory.[21]

Republicans Take Hawaii with Split Democrat Vote

Four days later, the Republicans won a special election in Hawaii that took some of the sting out of their loss in Pennsylvania. But the election of Republican Charles Djou, a Honolulu city councilman, to the district that Democratic representative Neil Abercrombie vacated to run for governor came with a major catch: Djou was on the ballot with two Democrats, state senator Colleen Hanabusa and former representative Ed Case, who split the Democratic vote and allowed Djou to win with a 40 percent plurality.

Still, Djou's fortuitous victory gave the Republicans a Democratic-held seat and did nothing to stop Republicans from claiming momentum.

Role of the Party Committees

The special elections in 2009 and 2010 highlighted the role that the six national party organizations will play in the midterm elections. They are the Democratic Congressional Campaign Committee (DCCC) and the National Republican Congressional Committee (NRCC), which work on House races; the Democratic Senatorial Campaign Committee (DSCC) and the National Republican Senatorial Committee (NRSC), which deal with Senate races; and the Democratic National Committee (DNC) and the Republican National Committee (RNC), which oversee overall party strategy, fund-raising, and voter registration efforts and also assist the House and Senate campaign committees.

In the midterm elections, the House and Senate campaign committees in particular work to recruit candidates and will spend millions of dollars on electronic and print communications and polling to help elect them.

The NRCC's candidate recruitment and training program, "Young Guns," ranks candidates in three levels: "On the Radar," "Contender," and, finally, "Young Gun."

"Candidates are named to the program by meeting individualized benchmarks set by the committee, which include developing grassroots support, fund-raising, and creating a media plan," the Capitol Hill newspaper *Roll Call* noted. "Those benchmarks become higher and more stringent with each level of the program."[22]

In February 2010 the NRCC announced the first ten candidates to reach the top "Young Guns" tier. By May 2010 the list of Young Guns had reached twenty-four candidates.[23]

Not all of those selected turned out to be top-notch candidates, however. Vaughn Ward, a Marine Corps veteran and former CIA official, was one of the NRCC's first ten Young Guns and was expected to easily secure the Republican nomination in Idaho's 1st district, where freshman Democratic representative Walt Minnick is seeking re-election.

But Ward was beset by serious problems in his campaign, most of them self-inflicted. It was revealed that he was delinquent in paying some property taxes and had filed an incomplete financial disclosure report, and his campaign plagiarized

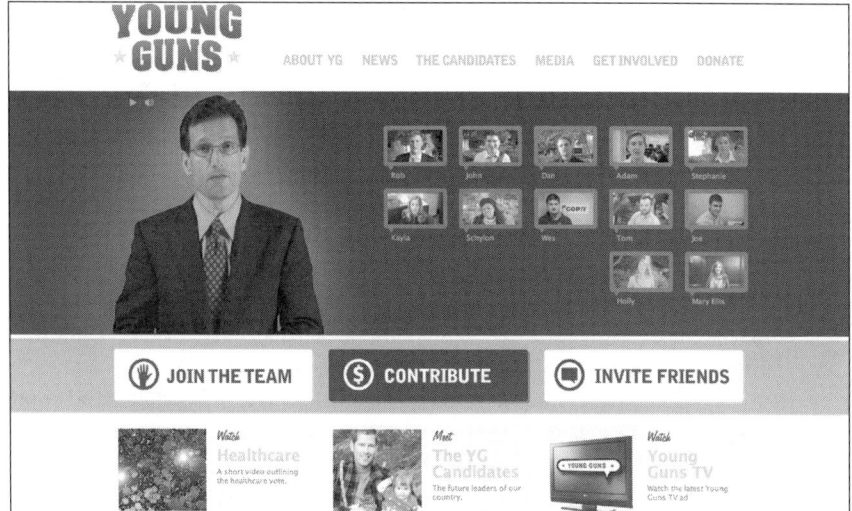

As it plots to win a majority of House seats in the 2010 election, the NRCC (the campaign arm of House Republicans) is promoting dozens of its preferred candidates in a recruitment and training program it calls "Young Guns." Candidates advance in the three-step program by meeting benchmarks in campaign fund-raising and organizational support. House minority leader Eric Cantor of Virginia, one of the program's three founders, is pictured above in a screenshot from the Young Guns Web site, www.gopyoungguns.com.

issue statements from the campaign Web sites of Republican members of Congress. In the end, Ward lost his primary election.

The DCCC has a "Frontline Democrats" program that delivers extra financial and logistical assistance to incumbents the committee sees as having the most difficult races. As of spring 2010, there were forty-two House Democrats enrolled in the program, many of them junior members from districts that lean more Republican than Democratic.

The DCCC also has a "Red to Blue" program under which it identifies and supports Democratic candidates trying to capture districts presently held by Republicans. The 2010 list of such candidates is rather small because there are so few districts left for Democrats to win after their large gains in the 2006 and 2008 elections.

Seven of the Democratic candidates are challenging Republican incumbents: Ami Bera, a physician challenging California representative Dan Lungren in the 3rd district near Sacramento; Paula Brooks, a county commissioner running against Ohio representative Pat Tiberi in the Columbus-area 12th district; John Callahan, the mayor of Bethlehem, Pennsylvania, taking on Rep. Charlie Dent in the Lehigh Valley–based 15th district; Suzan DelBene, a businesswoman and former Microsoft official running against Rep. Dave Reichert in the 8th district near Seattle, Washington; Rob Miller, a military veteran challenging Rep. Joe Wilson in a rematch of their competitive 2008 race in South Carolina's 2nd district; Steve Pougnet, the mayor of Palm Springs, taking on California representative Mary Bono Mack in the 44th district; and Tom White, a Nebraska state senator challenging Rep. Lee Terry in the Omaha-centered 2nd district.

Four others on the list are seeking seats that Republican incumbents are not defending: former Delaware lieutenant governor John Carney is running to succeed Rep. Michael N. Castle, a candidate for the Senate; Lori Edwards, a county elections supervisor in Florida is running to succeed Florida representative Adam Putnam, a candidate for state agriculture commissioner; Kansas state representative Raj Goyle is running to succeed Rep. Todd Tiahrt, a candidate for Senate; and in Illinois Dan Seals, a marketing executive and 2006 and 2008 candidate for the House, is running to succeed Rep. Mark Steven Kirk, a candidate for Senate.

Two other Democrats on the Red to Blue list actually are running to succeed other Democrats (and so their victories would not alter the partisan composition of the House): Pennsylvania state representative Bryan Lentz is running to succeed Rep. Joe Sestak, a candidate for the Senate; and Tennessee state senator Roy Herron is vying to succeed retiring Rep. John Tanner.

The DNC said in the spring of 2010 that it would spend at least $50 million to defend Democratic majorities in the House and Senate and win as many governorships and state legislative seats as possible.

About $30 million of these funds will go to voter registration, new media efforts, and other programs, and $20 million will be directed toward assisting candidates and committees in key races.

Democratic officials signaled that they intend to spend significant sums to engage and retain the support of the approximately fifteen million voters who cast their very first presidential votes for Barack Obama. Many of them are young African Americans and Latinos who belong to demographic groups that have below-average rates of voter turnout, especially in midterm elections.

"If we're able to increase their turnout from the norm even by 10 percent, that's a million and a half more votes that we could get," Kaine said.

Kaine said there are 400,000 such voters in Colorado, where there are key races for governor and senator; 750,000 in Ohio, where there are close contests for governor, senator, and in several House districts; and 1.3 million in Texas, where Democrats are eyeing the governorship.

"We know who these voters are, we know where they are, we know their loyalty to the president," Kaine said. "But the challenge that we're tackling, in, I think, a creative way, is getting them engaged in the midterm election in significant ways."[24]

Role of Outside Groups

The national party committees aren't the only noncandidate political organizations that will influence the midterm elections. Interest groups also will have a major say in who gets elected and defeated.

FIGURE 1
Voter Turnout in Presidential and Midterm Elections since World War II

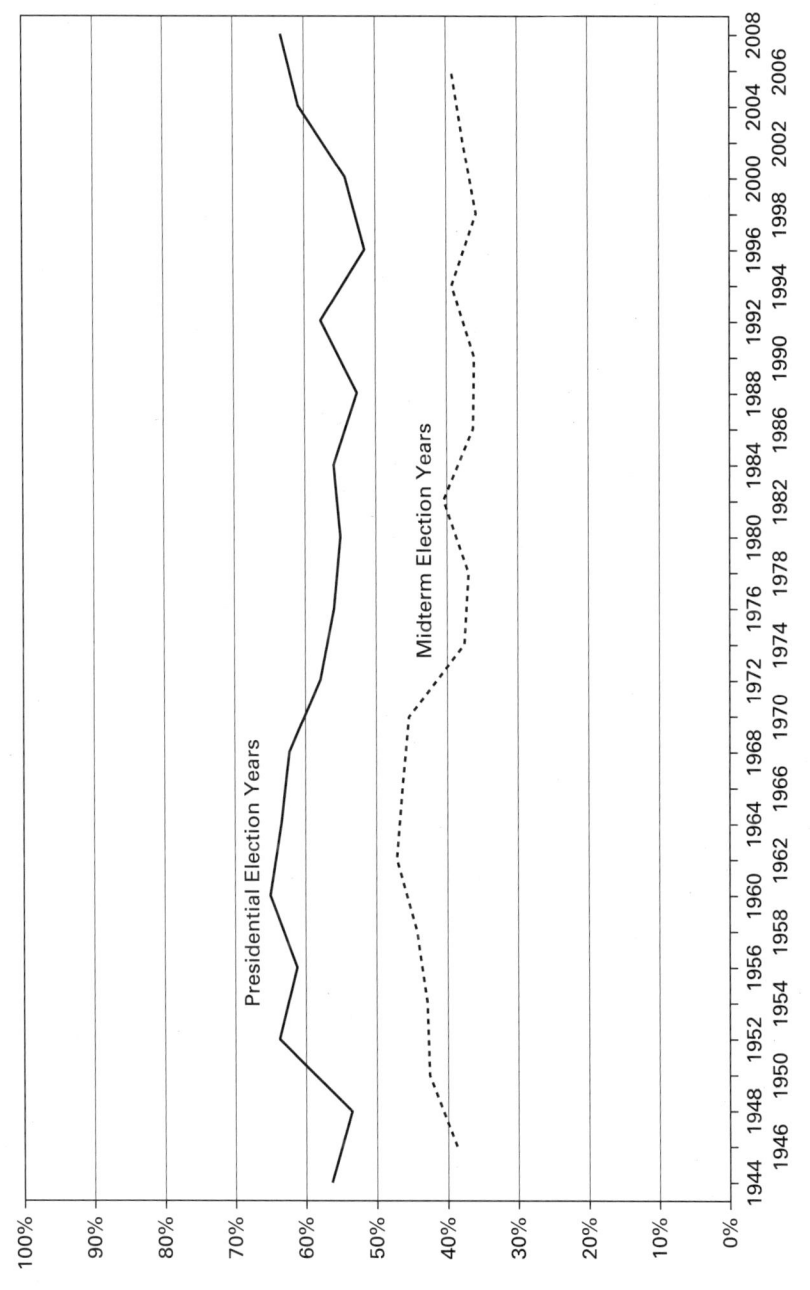

Source: Howard W. Stanley and Richard G. Niemi, *Vital Statistics on American Politics, 2009–2010* (Washington, D.C.: CQ Press, 2009).

The influential business federation the U.S. Chamber of Commerce will spend at least $50 million on the midterm elections, a 40 percent increase from 2008. It will target about ten Senate seats and forty House seats.[25] With its support of tax cuts, free trade, and restraint in spending, the Chamber supports more Republicans than Democrats but backs incumbents of both parties whose voting records it likes.

"We'll be there in the elections," said Thomas Donohue, the Chamber's chief executive officer. "With me, we support Democrats and Republicans. I get a lot of heat from some businesspeople for supporting important Democrats who vote with us. And I get heat from businesspeople for supporting, you know, too many Republicans."[26]

The National Rifle Association (NRA), which backs candidates who support gunowners' rights, plans to spend about $20 million on the elections through its political action committee.[27] Like many interest groups, the NRA issues a legislative scorecard that rates a lawmaker's or candidate's votes or positions on issues.

Another key player on the political right is the Club for Growth, which emphasizes such fiscally conservative policies as tax cuts, spending restraint, and free trade. Though it almost exclusively backs Republican candidates, the Club has ruffled some feathers in GOP circles because it doesn't shy away from opposing Republicans it sees as insufficiently conservative. For example, the Club for Growth vigorously opposed the re-nomination of Utah Republican senator Robert Bennett, in part because of his vote in 2008 for the Troubled Asset Relief Program (TARP), a plan to stabilize the financial markets that opponents denounced as an unnecessary and wasteful "bailout."

On the political left, labor unions will be working to corral votes for Democrats, particularly those who voted for the health care overhaul. The American Federation of State, County and Municipal Employees (AFSCME) and the Service Employees International Union (SEIU) are among the most powerful of these unions.

One of the more influential organizations on the political left is EMILY's List, which advises and raises money for Democratic women who support abortion rights. In the 2010 campaign cycle, it has endorsed and advised more than two dozen incumbents and candidates for House, Senate, and governor.

Other influential players include "527 organizations," political groups that get their name from the section of the federal tax code under which they are incorporated. These organizations engage in political activities and are often funded by large "soft money" political contributions that federal officeholders and national party committees no longer are permitted to raise.

One of the newest 527 groups is American Crossroads, a GOP group that is getting assistance from a constellation of GOP officials, including former RNC chair Ed Gillespie and former Bush senior adviser Karl Rove. The organization aims to raise $60 million.[28]

Then there is the vigorous anti-establishment movement of so-called tea party activists who have been showing up at town hall meetings, protests, and rallies to denounce excessive government spending, bailouts of large financial institutions, and the overhaul of health care policies. Though the tea party groups don't have a

A new phenomenon in the 2010 election is the emergence of a loose collection of so-called tea party activists who oppose excessive government spending, bailouts of large financial institutions, and the new health care law. In this photograph, tea party activists rally in Nashville, Tennessee, on April 15, 2009.

firm organizational structure and had limited political success in 2009 and early 2010, they could be a force in the midterm elections, mostly but not exclusively to the benefit of Republicans.

Republicans "love having the intensity on their side, but they're fearful of being associated with some of the elements of the tea party, and leaders who seem to be quite extreme, if not wacko," said Thomas E. Mann, a senior fellow at the Brookings Institution, a prominent think tank.[29]

The tea party movement did score a big coup in May 2010, though, when eye surgeon Rand Paul defeated Kentucky secretary of state Trey Grayson in a key Republican primary election in which Paul ran as an unabashed supporter of tea party priorities.

"I have a message from the Tea Party," Paul said at his victory party. "A message that is loud and clear and does not mince words: We have come to take our government back."

Interest groups and other nonparty organizations could play a larger role in the 2010 midterm elections in part because of a January 2010 Supreme Court ruling that loosened some restrictions on political spending. In a 5–4 decision, the Court's ruling in *Citizens United v. Federal Election Commission* loosened restrictions on how corporations, nonprofit organizations, and labor unions could spend money to influence federal elections during the height of the campaign season. The ruling did not overturn the ban on corporations and unions from donating directly to federal candidates.

"When government seeks to use its full power, including the criminal law, to command where a person may get his or her information or what distrusted source he or she may not hear, it uses censorship to control thought," Justice Anthony Kennedy wrote in the majority opinion. "This is unlawful. The First Amendment confirms the freedom to think for ourselves."

Several good-government groups denounced the ruling, saying that it would "open the door to the corrupting influence that would flow from such expenditures, as corporations and unions would use their spending, or the threat or promise of such spending, as a means to influence decision-making by Congress."[30]

President Obama even took the unusual step of criticizing the ruling at his annual State of the Union address just a few days after the Court's decision—and in the presence of the justices. "With all due deference to separation of powers," he said, "last week the Supreme Court reversed a century of law that I believe will open the floodgates for special interests, including foreign corporations, to spend without limit in our elections."

A few weeks later, in response to the Supreme Court ruling, some Democratic members of Congress announced legislation to regulate corporate and union spending. Rep. Chris Van Hollen of Maryland and Sen. Charles E. Schumer of New York said that their bill would bar expenditures by foreign-controlled corporations and from corporations that have received funds through TARP until after those funds are repaid. It would also bar election-related spending by federal contractors.

Opponents of campaign finance regulations denounced the bill. The Chamber's Donohue said that the bill is "aimed at one thing, and that's keeping the Chamber out of the midterm elections."[31]

Issues in the 2010 Election

It is an aphorism of elections that "good policy makes good politics." How well the majority Democrats and the Obama administration perform in this year's election will depend on how the voting public views their legislative accomplishments of the past two years.

The Economy

In early 2009, the Obama administration and the Democratic Congress initiated a burst of legislative activity that included an economic stimulus bill.

The economy clearly stood out as the biggest issue of concern. When Obama took office in January 2009, the unemployment rate was 8.5 percent, having risen steadily throughout 2008 as a financial and credit crisis took root. By large margins,

President Barack Obama and Sen. Barbara Boxer (D-Calif.) clasp hands and wave to supporters at a May 25, 2010, fund-raiser in San Francisco for Boxer and the DSCC. As head of the Democratic Party, Obama will campaign and raise money for Democratic members of Congress in difficult races.

according to Gallup surveys, the public identified either the "economy in general" or "unemployment/jobs" as the most important problem facing the country today.

In early 2009 Obama and Democrats moved to enact an economic recovery plan to jump-start the economy. What Obama signed into law in February 2009 was a $787 billion package that cut taxes for individuals and businesses and increased spending on health care, education, infrastructure, and energy, among other priorities. No Republicans in the U.S. House and just three GOP senators voted for the final measure, ensuring that this signature legislative accomplishment would become a partisan issue in the upcoming midterm elections.

President Obama defended his administration's economic policy in campaign stops across the country. At a May 2010 fund-raiser for California Democratic senator Barbara Boxer, Obama said, "We were on the brink of what many economists thought might be another Great Depression."

"And so we had to act quickly," the president said. "And that meant that right away we had to make sure that we put in place mechanisms to put people back to work, to get the economy growing again."[32]

Most Republicans denounced the economic recovery plan as a waste of money that exacerbated the deficit and did little to boost growth. Republicans noted that the unemployment rate in May 2010 was 9.7 percent, higher than when Obama took office.

Issues in the 2010 Election   25

Unlike Obama, GOP officeholders generally support extending the tax cuts enacted into law early in the administration of George W. Bush. Allowing the tax cuts to sunset, Republicans alleged, was tantamount to increasing taxes on the American people.

"Runaway spending is Washington's disease," Virginia Republican representative Eric Cantor, the House minority whip, said in April 2010. "The Democrats control every lever of power in Washington, and they've never met a tax they didn't like or found a dollar they couldn't spend. Their economic plan: you pay, they spend, and your children owe."[33]

In March 2010 Obama signed into law a $17.6 billion jobs bill—dubbed the Hiring Incentives to Restore Employment (HIRE) Act—that included a payroll tax break for businesses that hire jobless people and a $1,000 tax credit if these businesses keep those workers on the job at least a year.[34] Speaker Pelosi described the measure as "a very important piece of legislation," but Republicans countered that it wasn't deficit-neutral.[35]

Health Care Reform

Health care also will be a major issue in the 2010 elections. President Obama ran on a platform of universal health care coverage and reductions in health care costs. A bill he signed into law in March 2010 is aimed at expanding coverage to thirty-two million Americans in part by providing tax credits to businesses and subsidies to lower-income families.

Republicans denounced the measure as a government "takeover" of the health care industry. They vowed to make health care an issue in the midterm elections and said they would repeal most if not all of the measure if they captured legislative majorities. "Repeal and replace" became a frequent Republican talking point.

"The November election is clearly going to be a referendum on this issue," said South Dakota senator John Thune. "Depending on how it comes out, our efforts will be to repeal and replace."[36]

Though polls in spring 2010 showed that more people disliked than liked the health care bill, Democrats practically dared Republicans to promise to repeal a measure that they said would become more popular over time once people learned about all of the plan's benefits.

"This is the reform that some folks in Washington are still hollering about, still shouting about," Obama said in Iowa a few days after the bill signing. "Now that they passed it—now that we passed it—they're already promising to repeal it. They're actually going to run on a platform of repeal in November. You've been hearing that. And my attitude is: Go for it."[37]

Other Issues

The Democrats plan to run on a platform of tightening regulations on the financial institutions that contributed to the ongoing economic woes of the United States. In December 2009 the House passed a financial regulatory bill, and the Senate passed

President Barack Obama signs the health care bill into law in the East Room of the White House on March 23, 2010, as Vice President Joseph Biden, House Speaker Nancy Pelosi, Senate Majority Leader Harry Reid, and other Democratic luminaries look on. Health care reform was the president's top domestic policy priority.

its version in May 2010. A conference committee of House members and senators began meeting in June to iron out differences in the bills.

The Obama administration and members of Congress also may have to grapple with the political fallout of a massive oil spill caused by the explosion and sinking of an offshore deep-sea oil rig in the Gulf of Mexico in late April 2010. That massive environmental disaster, coupled with the public's dislike of how both the government and energy company BP handled the cleanup efforts, sparked speculation that the oil spill would be "Obama's Katrina," a reference to the 2005 hurricane that decimated New Orleans and surrounding areas. The government's uneven response to that crisis hurt President George W. Bush's image one year before his party was trounced that the polls in the 2006 midterm elections.

According to an ABC News/*Washington Post* poll in early June 2010, 69 percent of respondents rated the federal response to the oil spill negatively. That compares to a 62 percent negative rating two weeks after Katrina.[38]

While domestic issues almost certainly will dominate the attention of most voters, national security always is an abiding concern nine years after the September 2001 terrorist attacks and with more than one hundred thousand U.S. troops fighting wars in Iraq and Afghanistan. An uptick in U.S. troop casualties abroad or some major international conflagration could make foreign policy a front-burner issue.

Key Senate Races

Republicans began the 2010 election cycle facing near insuperable odds to regain a majority in the Senate. At the start of 2009, the Democrats held fifty-nine seats after making a net gain of eight seats in the 2008 election. The Democrats acquired a sixtieth seat in April 2009 when Sen. Arlen Specter left the Republican Party to become a Democrat, though Republicans offset that in January 2010 with the election of Republican Scott Brown to the Massachusetts seat previously held by the late Democratic senator Edward M. Kennedy.

Though the opposition party almost always makes gains in midterm elections, in the early months of the 2010 cycle it appeared that the Democrats might actually augment their majority by one or more seats. In December 2008, one month after the Democratic landslides, Republican senator Mel Martinez of Florida announced that he would not run for a second term. One month later, Republican senator Christopher S. Bond of Missouri announced his retirement, and this was followed four days later by a similar announcement from Republican senator George V. Voinovich. Florida and Ohio had voted for Obama in 2008, and Missouri voted narrowly for John McCain.

"A rash of retirements among Senate Republicans plus difficult re-election prospects for several incumbents has boosted the Democrats' chances to enlarge their majority beyond sixty seats next year for the first time since 1977," journalist Donald Lambro wrote in mid-January 2009.[39]

But Republicans got some key breaks in late 2009 and early 2010. Strong candidates like Illinois representative Mark Steven Kirk and Delaware representative Michael N. Castle give Republicans an excellent chance to win the seats formerly held by President Obama and Vice President Biden. And the unexpected retirements of Democratic senators Byron L. Dorgan of North Dakota and Evan Bayh of Indiana also worked to the Republicans' advantage.

Republicans aren't expecting to win a majority of Senate seats this year. But if they make robust gains, they could position themselves to win a majority in 2012, when twenty-three Democrats and ten Republicans will be defending their seats. So the GOP will have more seats to target and fewer to defend than in 2010.

Democratic-Held States

Arkansas. Sen. Blanche Lincoln was in perilous political condition in early 2010. Republicans planned to vigorously contest her re-election in a conservative-leaning state where President Obama is not popular, but she also faced a serious challenge to her renomination from Lt. Gov. Bill Halter, who ran with the support of labor unions and liberal groups angry with Lincoln over some of her votes on health care and other issues. Lincoln managed to narrowly defeat Halter in a June runoff election, 52 percent to 48 percent, but she trailed Republican representative John Boozman in early general election polls.

California. Sen. Barbara Boxer, a strident liberal, is expected to face a serious race in her state. Three very different Republicans emerged to challenge Boxer: Tom Campbell, a moderate former House member (1989–1993, 1995–2001) from Silicon Valley who lost Senate races in 1992 and 2000; Carly Fiorina, the former chief executive officer of Hewlett-Packard; and Chuck DeVore, a member of the state Assembly who ran as the most conservative Republican of the group. Campbell led in Republican polls for most of the race but was overtaken by Fiorina, who spent millions of her own money to fund television ads. Early polls of the general election had Boxer as a slight favorite over Fiorina in California's first statewide congressional race in which a woman is the nominee for both major parties.

Colorado. Sen. Michael Bennet is seeking a full term after being appointed in January 2009 to succeed Ken Salazar, who became President Obama's interior secretary. Bennet is facing a tough race because he isn't well known statewide, and it's a difficult time to be an incumbent.

Bennet faces opposition in the August Democratic primary from Andrew Romanoff, a former state House Speaker who has forsworn contributions from political action committees (PACs).

The White House is backing Bennet, a former Denver schools superintendent whom Obama seriously considered for the post of education secretary. But the lengths to which the White House was prepared to discourage Romanoff from running were on full display in June 2010, when Romanoff disclosed that senior Obama aide Jim Messina e-mailed him to suggest three jobs that might be available to Romanoff if he were not running for the Senate.

The main contenders for the Republican nomination are former lieutenant governor Jane Norton and county prosecutor Ken Buck. Norton is the preferred candidate of the Republican establishment, whereas Buck has drawn support from tea party activists.

Connecticut. The retirement announcement of Sen. Christopher J. Dodd in early January 2010 actually improved Democratic prospects of retaining the seat because Dodd had poor approval ratings and the party had a strong prospect waiting in the wings, popular state attorney general Richard Blumenthal. Democrats nominated him at a convention in May.

A crowded field developed on the Republican side even before Dodd announced he would not run again. The early front-runner seemed to be Rob Simmons, a former House member, but he withdrew from the race after he was outpolled at a convention by Linda McMahon, the wealthy former chief executive officer of World Wrestling Entertainment (WWE) who spent lavishly on her campaign.

The Connecticut Senate race garnered national headlines in mid-May, when the *New York Times* reported that Blumenthal had misled crowds into thinking that he served in Vietnam when he was actually stationed stateside during that conflict. Blumenthal acknowledged that he misspoke and later apologized, and the issue didn't appear to hurt his campaign all that much.

TABLE 2
Senators Up in 2010

Republican-held seats (18)

State	Senator	First Elected	Last Win %	2008 President	2004 President
Alabama	Richard C. Shelby	1986 (4th term)	68%	McCain, 60%–39%	Bush, 62%–37%
Alaska	Lisa Murkowski	2004 (1st full term)	48%	McCain, 59%–38%	Bush, 61%–36%
Arizona	John McCain	1986 (4th term)	77%	McCain, 54%–45%	Bush, 55%–44%
Florida	George LeMieux (retiring)	2009 (appointed)		Obama, 51%–48%	Bush, 52%–47%
Georgia	Johnny Isakson	2004 (1st term)	58%	McCain, 52%–47%	Bush, 58%–41%
Idaho	Michael Crapo	1998 (2nd term)	99%	McCain, 62%–36%	Bush, 68%–30%
Iowa	Charles E. Grassley	1980 (5th term)	70%	Obama, 54%–45%	Bush, 50%–49%
Kansas	Sam Brownback (retiring)	1996 (2nd full term)	69%	McCain, 57%–42%	Bush, 62%–37%
Kentucky	Jim Bunning (retiring)	1998 (2nd term)	51%	McCain, 57%–41%	Bush, 60%–40%
Louisiana	David Vitter	2004 (1st term)	51%	McCain, 59%–40%	Bush, 57%–42%
Missouri	Christopher S. Bond (retiring)	1986 (4th term)	56%	McCain, 49.4%–49.3%	Bush, 53%–46%
New Hampshire	Judd Gregg (retiring)	1992 (3rd term)	66%	Obama, 54%–45%	Kerry, 50%–49%
North Carolina	Richard M. Burr	2004 (1st term)	52%	Obama, 49.7%–49.4%	Bush, 56%–44%
Ohio	George V. Voinovich (retiring)	1998 (2nd term)	64%	Obama, 52%–47%	Bush, 51%–49%
Oklahoma	Tom Coburn	2004 (1st term)	53%	McCain, 66%–34%	Bush, 66%–34%
South Carolina	Jim DeMint	2004 (1st term)	54%	McCain, 54%–45%	Bush, 58%–41%
South Dakota	John Thune	2004 (1st term)	51%	McCain, 53%–45%	Bush, 60%–38%
Utah	Robert F. Bennett*	1992 (3rd term)	69%	McCain, 63%–34%	Bush, 72%–26%

*Bennett was defeated for renomination at a convention in May 2010.

Democratic–held seats (18)

State	Senator	First Elected	Last Win %	2008 President	2004 President
Arkansas	Blanche Lincoln	1998 (2nd term)	56%	McCain, 59%–39%	Bush, 54%–45%
California	Barbara Boxer	1992 (3rd term)	58%	Obama, 61%–37%	Kerry, 54%–44%
Colorado	Michael Bennet	2009 (appointed)		Obama, 54%–45%	Bush, 52%–47%
Connecticut	Christopher Dodd (retiring)	1980 (5th term)	66%	Obama, 61%–38%	Kerry, 54%–44%
Delaware	Ted Kaufman (retiring)	2009 (appointed)		Obama, 62%–37%	Kerry, 53%–46%
Hawaii	Daniel K. Inouye	1962 (8th term)	76%	Obama, 72%–27%	Kerry, 54%–45%
Illinois	Roland W. Burris (retiring)	2009 (appointed)		Obama, 62%–37%	Kerry, 55%–44%
Indiana	Evan Bayh (retiring)	1998 (2nd term)	62%	Obama, 50%–49%	Bush, 60%–39%
Maryland	Barbara A. Mikulski	1986 (4th term)	65%	Obama, 62%–36%	Kerry, 56%–43%
Nevada	Harry Reid	1986 (4th term)	61%	Obama, 55%–43%	Bush, 50%–48%
New York	Charles E. Schumer	1998 (2nd term)	71%	Obama, 63%–36%	Kerry, 58%–40%
New York	Kirsten E. Gillibrand	2009 (appointed)		Obama, 63%–36%	Kerry, 58%–40%
North Dakota	Byron L. Dorgan (retiring)	1992 (3rd term)	68%	McCain, 53%–45%	Bush, 63%–35%
Oregon	Ron Wyden	1996 (2nd full term)	63%	Obama, 57%–40%	Kerry, 51%–47%
Pennsylvania	Arlen Specter*	1980 (5th term)	53%	Obama, 55%–44%	Kerry, 51%–48%
Vermont	Patrick J. Leahy	1974 (6th term)	71%	Obama, 67%–30%	Kerry, 59%–39%
Washington	Patty Murray	1992 (3rd term)	55%	Obama, 58%–40%	Kerry, 53%–46%
Wisconsin	Russ Feingold	1992 (3rd term)	55%	Obama, 56%–42%	Kerry, 50%–49%

Source: Howard W. Stanley and Richard G. Niemi, *Vital Statistics on American Politics, 2009–2010* (Washington, D.C.: CQ Press, 2009).

*Specter announced April 28, 2009, that he would seek re-election as a Democrat rather than as a Republican. He was defeated in the Democratic primary on May 18, 2010.

Delaware. Republicans are strongly favored to capture the Senate seat that Biden vacated in early 2009 as he prepared to assume the vice presidency. Biden was re-elected to the Senate on the same day he was elected vice president, and so a special election will be held in November 2010 to determine who will serve the remaining four years of the term he won.

To replace Biden in the interim, outgoing Democratic governor Ruth Ann Minner announced that she would appoint Ted Kaufman, Biden's former chief of staff, as a temporary "placeholder" who would not run for election in 2010. The idea was to not show favoritism to any candidate.

At the time, it was widely assumed that Biden's eldest son, state attorney general Beau Biden, would run for the seat and give Democrats a good chance of defending it.

As Beau Biden was weighing his decision, the Republicans scored a coup when Republican representative Michael N. Castle announced in early October 2009 that he would run for the Senate. Castle is a popular former governor who has not lost an election in a political career spanning four decades and who is a household name in Delaware.

Biden unexpectedly announced in late January that he would not run. The stated reason was that he wanted to devote his professional energies to the prosecution of an infamous pedophile.

Democrats turned next to Chris Coons, an ambitious young executive of government operations in populous New Castle County, which includes Wilmington. Early polls gave Castle a large lead, but even he suggested that the race would become close.

Illinois. An even bigger symbolic victory for Republicans than winning Vice President Biden's seat in Delaware would be capturing the seat formerly held by President Obama. The interim seatholder is Roland Burris, who doomed any chance he had to become a viable candidate for election when he accepted the position from then governor Rod Blagojevich, who would later be impeached and accused of numerous scandals.

The winners of the February 2010 primaries were Republican representative Mark Steven Kirk and Democratic state treasurer Alexi Giannoulias. The general Democratic lean of Illinois will help Giannoulias, but Kirk's Republican centrism should play well in key suburban areas. Giannoulias narrowly trailed Kirk in the polls in the spring, in part because he was hampered by allegations concerning loans his family's bank made to some unsavory individuals.

Indiana. Democratic senator Evan Bayh seemed headed for an easy victory for a third term—until former senator Dan Coats announced in early February that he would seek the seat he had held from 1989 through 1998, when he retired and was succeeded by Bayh.

In mid-February, to the great surprise of just about everyone, Bayh announced that he would not stand for re-election. Because he made his announcement on the eve of the candidate filing deadline, no Democrat qualified for the May primary ballot. Under state law, party officials chose Rep. Brad Ellsworth, a popular moderate from the southwestern part of the state, as the Democratic nominee. He'll face Coats, who won a five-candidate primary with 39 percent of the vote.

Race to Watch **Nevada.** Senate majority leader Harry Reid was in dire political straits in early 2010 in part because of his state's poor economy and the difficult political environment. Early polls showed him trailing multiple GOP contenders.

Reid denied that his leadership position detracted from his focus on Nevada. "I think when, you know . . . the accounting's done on the books, you'll find that my role as Majority Leader has been very, very good for Nevada," Reid said. "I control what goes in and out of the Senate, and as a result of that Nevada's gotten far more than its share."[40]

One bright spot for Reid is that several well-known Republicans, including former representative Jon Porter, declined to challenge him, and the field of GOP contenders that did form wasn't all that strong. The winner of the Republican primary was Sharron Angle, a former state assemblywoman who ran with support from tea party activists and also had the backing of the conservative Club for Growth.

A Senate majority leader was last defeated for re-election in 1952, when Arizona Democrat Ernest McFarland was felled by Republican Barry Goldwater (who would be the 1964 Republican nominee for president).

North Dakota. No seat is more likely to change in partisan control than the one in North Dakota. Democratic senator Byron Dorgan surprisingly announced in January 2010 that he would not defend his seat for re-election. Dorgan might have been opposed by Republican governor John Hoeven, a highly popular chief executive who entered the race shortly after Dorgan exited it. The Democratic nominee is state senator Tracy Potter, who trailed Hoeven by more than 40 percentage points in spring polls.

Pennsylvania. At the beginning of 2009, Sen. Arlen Specter was a moderate-to-liberal Republican facing a serious challenge in the primary election from Pat Toomey, a conservative former congressman who had nearly beaten Specter in a 2004 primary. Specter's vote for an economic recovery plan promoted by the Obama administration only further inflamed the anger of Republican primary voters in Pennsylvania.

As a result, in late April 2009, Specter announced that he was switching parties and becoming a Democrat, mainly because "the prospects for winning a Republican primary are bleak." He said he was not prepared to have his fate determined by a "Pennsylvania Republican primary electorate."

Specter's party switch gave Democrats an operational sixty-seat majority in the Senate and was hailed by President Obama and the Democratic Senatorial Campaign Committee, which promised to support him.

But Specter's party switch struck many longtime Democratic voters as opportunistic, and the party establishment was unable to secure Specter a clear path to the Democratic nomination. He was challenged by Rep. Joe Sestak, a two-term

An Anti-Incumbent Year?

Bennett

Mollohan

Specter and wife Joan

A toxic political environment in 2010 prompted many political analysts to declare that the election year would be a bad one for congressional incumbents. At the midpoint of the year, though, the evidence was mixed.

Public approval of Congress was at or near an all-time low, and many Americans continued to be disgusted with what they saw as an inability by policymakers to tackle the nation's most pressing problems.

Months before the November voting, a handful of members of Congress were bounced from office in primary elections. The first was Utah Republican senator Robert Bennett, who placed third in an unusual nominating convention in early May, a victim of conservative anger at his 2008 vote to stabilize the financial markets and his stance on several other policy positions.

Just three days after Bennett lost, West Virginia Democratic representative Alan B. Mollohan was trounced in a primary by state senator Mike Oliverio, who made Mollohan's unethical behavior while in office a centerpiece of his campaign.

One week after that, on May 18, Republican-turned-Democratic senator Arlen Specter was felled in a primary by Democratic representative Joe Sestak, who cast Specter's party switch a year earlier as an exercise in political expediency.

On June 1, another party-switcher went down in defeat: Democratic-turned-Republican representative Parker Griffith of Alabama didn't come close to convincing a majority of voters in his adopted party that he was really one of them.

Still, in a counterpoint to the anti-incumbent narrative, other incumbents seen as vulnerable in primary elections hung on to win. Among these was Arkansas Democratic senator Blanche Lincoln, who needed a runoff election to win renomination against Lt. Gov. Bill Halter. Many political analysts thought that Lincoln would lose the runoff after a mediocre showing in the first-round primary election, but she recovered to win. Still, she may lose the general election in her conservative-leaning state.

It remains to be seen whether the voting public's general disenchantment with Congress will translate into huge losses in November for officeholders in one or both parties—or if once again 90 percent or more of members of Congress will be returned to office, albeit with somewhat smaller margins of victory. Incumbency still is a powerful force in elections, even in turbulent election years.

congressman from the Philadelphia suburbs who ran a well-funded campaign in which he portrayed himself as "the Democrat" in the race. Specter defended his seniority as helpful to Pennsylvania.

In the May 2010 primary election, Sestak defeated Specter, 54 percent to 46 percent. He will face Toomey in the fall in a contest that polls suggest will be very competitive.

Washington. Three-term senator Patty Murray faced the prospect of a competitive race from Dino Rossi, a former state senator who ran strong but losing campaigns for governor in 2004 and 2008.

Wisconsin. Three-term senator Russ Feingold almost certainly will square off against Republican Ron Johnson, a wealthy businessman who entered the race in May 2010, a few weeks after Republican former governor Tommy Thompson declined to enter a race that would have been a titanic battle. Johnson could still give Feingold a run for his money, in part because of the personal resources that he can bring to bear.

Republican-Held States

Florida. Popular Republican governor Charlie Crist initially appeared to be a shoo-in for the seat of Republican senator Mel Martinez, who announced his retirement in December 2008 and resigned from the Senate in September 2009.

But Crist faced determined opposition for the Republican nomination from Marco Rubio, a young former state House Speaker who claimed that Crist wasn't as conservative as he claimed to be. Rubio pointed to Crist's support of President Obama's economic recovery law as support for his claims.

Conservative groups and blogs rallied behind Rubio, who eventually overtook Crist in the polls and effectively forced the governor to announce in April 2010 that he would run for the Senate as an independent.

The Democratic nominee will either be Rep. Kendrick Meek or wealthy real estate developer Jeff Greene.

Kentucky. It's rare for an incumbent's retirement to improve the defending party's chances of retaining a seat. But Republican officials actually breathed a sigh of relief when two-term senator Jim Bunning, who struggled to raise money and who had a poor public image in his state, announced that he would not be seeking re-election.

In the Republican race to succeed Bunning, party leaders in Washington, D.C., including Senate minority leader Mitch McConnell of Kentucky, preferred Kentucky secretary of state Trey Grayson.

But Grayson could not reasonably expect to have an automatic "in" in a good Republican year and in a conservative-leaning state. As expected, several other Republicans jumped into the race, most notably Rand Paul from Bowling Green, a first-time candidate for political office and the son of Texas Republican representative Ron Paul, who drew a devoted following in his quixotic bid for the 2008 Republican presidential nomination.

Tea party activists across the nation assisted Paul's efforts. He trounced Grayson, 59 percent to 35 percent, and he will face Kentucky Democratic attorney general Jack

Conway in a November election that should be among the nation's most closely watched contests.

Louisiana. Sen. David Vitter was vulnerable to losing his seat in no small part because of his entanglement in a D.C. sex scandal. That most likely won't be enough, however, to unseat the senator in a state that has been trending Republican and in a year in which the GOP is expected to make gains.

The Democrats have a good candidate, though, in Rep. Charlie Melancon, a moderately conservative Democrat who is in his third term representing a conservative-leaning district in the southeastern part of the state.

Missouri. The decision by Republican senator Christopher S. "Kit" Bond to decline a re-election campaign essentially guaranteed a competitive race in a state known for its taut partisan equilibrium. Most of the Senate races in Missouri over the past twenty years have been decided by single digits.

The likely November matchup materialized more than a year before the election. The Democrats quickly rallied behind Missouri secretary of state Robin Carnahan, a member of the state's most prominent political family (she's the daughter of the late governor Mel Carnahan and former senator Jean Carnahan). Ten Republicans sought the GOP nomination, but by far the leading candidate is Rep. Roy Blunt, a seven-term member from the southwestern part of the state.

Republicans portrayed Carnahan as too liberal for Missouri and branded her as "Rubberstamp Robin" on the grounds that she would side reflexively with the positions of President Obama and Democratic leaders. Democrats planned to remind voters of Blunt's service as a House Republican leader during the presidency of George W. Bush and his close ties to and frequent political contributions from lobbyists.

New Hampshire. Republican senator Judd Gregg surely would have been easily re-elected had he chosen to seek a fourth term in 2010, but his retirement gave Democrats an opportunity to win his seat in a state where they scored some high-profile victories in the 2006 and 2008 elections.

Democrats quickly rallied behind Rep. Paul W. Hodes, who is serving his second term representing the western half of the state. The Republican primary was more wide open: Republican officials in Washington, D.C., preferred Kelly Ayotte, a former state attorney general, though she faced determined and wealthy opposition in businessmen Jim Bender and Bill Binnie and also from political activist Ovide Lamontagne.

North Carolina. Sen. Richard Burr is seeking a second term to a seat to which no senator has been re-elected in more than forty years.[41] However, he seemed likely to be re-elected over either of two Democrats, Secretary of State Elaine Marshall or lawyer Cal Cunningham, who was the preferred candidate of the DSCC.

Race to Watch **Ohio.** The retirement of Republican senator George V. Voinovich guaranteed a competitive open-seat race in a quintessential political battleground.

Republican Rob Portman, a former Cincinnati-area congressman who later became a top budget and trade official to President George W. Bush, sought the seat and caught a break when Tom Ganley, a wealthy car dealer, decided against challenging Portman for the Republican nomination.

On the Democratic side, the contestants were Lt. Gov. Lee Fisher and Ohio secretary of state Jennifer Brunner. The Democratic establishment backed Fisher in large part because he raised far more money than Brunner, who eschewed a traditional media-heavy campaign and concentrated instead on reaching out to left-leaning blogs and activists.

Portman and Fisher began sparring on the issues of the economy and jobs months before they won their respective nominations. Portman criticized Fisher's record as lieutenant governor, and Fisher described Portman as an architect of Bush's economic policies.

Conservative Discontent. Some other races are notable not for the general election they may produce but for their primary elections.

In Arizona, Sen. John McCain, the 2008 Republican presidential nominee, will be challenged in the August primary election by former representative J. D. Hayworth, who represented the Tempe and Scottsdale area from 1995 through 2006, when he was defeated for re-election in that year's Democratic upswing.

Hayworth hoped to tap into conservatives' discontent with McCain, who long cultivated an image as a political "maverick" with his support for campaign finance reform and legislation to combat global warming and allow some illegal immigrants to earn citizenship.

After losing to Obama, McCain's voting record became much more in line with those of the Republican leaders; a Congressional Quarterly study found that in 2009 McCain voted more frequently with his party on closely divided votes than in any other year of his career.[42] Perhaps the senator anticipated that he might have to withstand a challenge to his right flank.

But McCain told *Newsweek* magazine in early April, "I never considered myself a maverick. I consider myself a person who serves the people of Arizona to the best of his abilities."[43]

These comments drew surprised reactions in many quarters, including the Pulitzer Prize–winning fact-checking and statement-vetting site Politifact.com, which documented several instances in which McCain referred to himself as a maverick in public appearances or in campaign ads.[44]

Democrats have no chance of winning the Senate seat in Utah, one of the nation's most strongly Republican states. But there will be a new GOP senator there after the defeat of Republican senator Robert F. Bennett at a party convention in May 2010.

Key House Races

Republicans also planned to make a pitched effort to make major gains in the U.S. House of Representatives and perhaps even secure a majority of seats. It would not be easy.

As of June 2010, the Democrats held 255 seats and Republicans held 177 seats, with vacancies in two districts previously held by Republicans and one held by a Democrat. So, if the vacant districts are assigned to the parties that most recently held them, then the Republicans would need a net gain of 39 seats to win a majority of 218 seats.

Still, Republican officials have set their sights high. Texas representative Pete Sessions, chair of the NRCC, said in April 2010 that anything less than winning a majority of seats "is a warm bucket of spit."[45]

Other Republican-allied groups, however, suggested that the party would not make the net gain of thirty-nine House seats to win back the majority.

"I suspect there will be a fair amount of turnover, but it would be a long reach to take back the House," said Tom Donohue of the Chamber of Commerce in late May 2010.[46]

But there are dozens of Democratic districts where the Republicans will wage vigorous takeover campaigns. They include the forty-nine districts that voted Republican for president but elected or re-elected a Democrat to the House.[47] Many of these districts are represented by junior Democrats that the DCCC has included among the forty-two members on its "Frontline Democrats" list.

There will be competitive House races all over the country, though the Midwest will be a key battleground. Here are some of key states that will hold multiple competitive contests:

Indiana. Democrats won three seats from the Republicans in the 2006 election that the GOP is eager to win back. They are the South Bend–based 2nd district, where two-term Democratic representative Joe Donnelly will face Republican state representative Jackie Walorski; the Evansville-area 8th district, where Democratic state representative Trent Van Haaften will face Republican physician Larry Bucshon for the seat of Democratic representative Brad Ellsworth, a candidate for the Senate; and the southeastern 9th district, where Democratic representative Baron Hill will be vigorously challenged by Republican lawyer Todd Young.

Race to Watch **Ohio.** Republicans will be looking to defeat Democratic representatives Steve Driehaus of the Cincinnati-area 1st district, Mary Jo Kilroy of the Columbus-based 15th district, John Boccieri of the Canton-area 16th district, and Zack Space of the east central 18th district. Driehaus, Kilroy, and Boccieri are freshmen, and Space is seeking his second term.

Race to Watch **Pennsylvania.** According to June 2010 ratings of House races maintained by Congressional Quarterly and Roll Call, no state will have more competitive contests than Pennsylvania, with ten.[48] Top targets for the Republican Party include Democratic representatives Kathy Dahlkemper of the Erie-based 3rd district, Paul E. Kanjorski of the Scranton-area 11th district, and Mark Critz of the southwestern 12th district. Republicans also have a good shot at winning the suburban Philadelphia-based 7th district that Democratic representative Joe Sestak is giving up to run for the Senate.

Key Gubernatorial Races

About three-fourths of the nation's governors are elected in midterm election years. A large number of gubernatorial races should be highly competitive this year, in part because of the anti-incumbent political environment but also because so many governors were term-limited or chose not to seek re-election.

The governor's races assumed added urgency this year because of the implications for the congressional redistricting process in 2011 and 2012. In most states, governors get to sign or veto redistricting maps, just like any other bill.

This year's gubernatorial elections also are notable in that five former governors are running to reclaim their former jobs—Republicans Terry E. Branstad of Iowa and Robert L. Ehrlich Jr. of Maryland and Democrats Roy Barnes of Georgia, Jerry Brown of California, and John Kitzhaber of Oregon.

"While no group keeps official statistics, experts in both parties said they could not recall a time when so many individuals sought to recapture the governor's seat in one election year," the *New York Times* reported in November 2009. "With 37 seats up for grabs in 2010, these old newcomers have introduced an unusual dynamic as both parties scramble to pick up new states."[49]

Democratic-Held Seats

Colorado. Gov. Bill Ritter announced his retirement in February 2010 amid mediocre poll ratings, and Denver mayor John Hickenlooper planned to run in his stead. Republicans planned to choose either former representative Scott McInnis or businessman Dan Maes, a favorite of tea party activists.

Illinois. It won't be easy for Gov. Pat Quinn to win an election in his own right this year. The state's fiscal situation is not good, and Republicans will try to link Quinn to disgraced former governor Rod Blagojevich, whose impeachment and removal from office in early 2009 elevated Quinn from the lieutenant governorship. His Republican opponent is Bill Brady, a state senator from downstate.

Iowa. Gov. Chet Culver, who is seeking a second term, will face a difficult re-election campaign against Terry Branstad, the state's Republican governor from 1983 through 1998.

Kansas. Gov. Kathleen Sebelius was barred by term limits from seeking re-election when President Obama tapped her in early 2009 to run the federal Health and Human Services Department. Mark Parkinson, who was elevated from the lieutenant governorship upon Sebelius's resignation, was eligible to seek a full term but he declined to do so. Given the state's Republican proclivities, and a strong candidate in Sen. Sam Brownback, it's likely that the governorship will flip from Democratic to Republican.

TABLE 3
Governors Up in 2010

State	Governor, Party
Alabama	Bob Riley, R*
Alaska	Sean Parnell, R
Arizona	Jan Brewer, R
Arkansas	Mike Beebe, D
California	Arnold Schwarzenegger, R*
Colorado	Bill Ritter, D*
Connecticut	Jodi Rell, R*
Florida	Charlie Crist, R*
Georgia	Sonny Perdue, R*
Hawaii	Linda Lingle, R*
Idaho	C.L. "Butch" Otter, R
Illinois	Pat Quinn, D
Iowa	Chet Culver, D
Kansas	Mark Parkinson, D*
Maine	John Baldacci, D*
Maryland	Martin O'Malley, D
Massachusetts	Deval Patrick, D
Michigan	Jennifer Granholm, D*
Minnesota	Tim Pawlenty, R*
Nebraska	Dave Heineman, R
Nevada	Jim Gibbons, R**
New Hampshire	John Lynch, D
New Mexico	Bill Richardson, D*
New York	David Paterson, D*
Ohio	Ted Strickland, D
Oklahoma	Brad Henry, D*
Oregon	Ted Kulongoski, D*
Pennsylvania	Ed Rendell, D*
Rhode Island	Don Carcieri, R*
South Carolina	Mark Sanford, R*
South Dakota	Mike Rounds, R*
Tennessee	Phil Bredesen, D*
Texas	Rick Perry, R
Utah	Gary Herbert, R
Vermont	Jim Douglas, R*
Wisconsin	Jim Doyle, D*
Wyoming	Dave Freudenthal, D*

Source: Compiled by author.
*not seeking re-election
**defeated in primary

Maine. Gov. John Baldacci is term-limited in 2010 and a large field of would-be successors in both parties lined up to succeed him. The November contestants will be Democratic state Senate president Elizabeth "Libby" Mitchell and Republican Waterville mayor Paul LePage.

Maryland. The race between Gov. Martin O'Malley and former governor Robert L. Ehrlich Jr. will be a rematch of a 2006 contest that O'Malley won by seven percentage points.

Massachusetts. Gov. Deval Patrick's mediocre approval ratings mean that he will have to fight hard for a second term in his normally Democratic-leaning state. Charlie Baker, a businessman and former gubernatorial aide, will be the Republican nominee. State treasurer Tim Cahill, who was elected to his post as a Democrat, is running as an independent.

Race to Watch ***Michigan.*** Gov. Jennifer Granholm is term-limited in 2010. The two Democrats vying for the nomination are Lansing mayor Virg Bernero, a populist Democrat, and state House Speaker Andy Dillon, who is more moderate. The large Republican field includes Rep. Pete Hoekstra, state attorney general Mike Cox, Oakland County sheriff Mike Bouchard, state senator Tom George, and businessman Rick Snyder.

New Mexico. Gov. Bill Richardson is term-limited in 2010 and Democratic lieutenant governor Diane Denish will be her party's nominee. She'll face Republican Susana Martinez, a county prosecutor, in a race that will produce the first woman governor in New Mexico's history.

New York. Gov. David Paterson, who was elevated from the lieutenant governorship upon the March 2008 resignation of Eliot Spitzer in a prostitution scandal, announced in February 2010 that he would not seek a term in his own right. Paterson received poor marks from the public for his performance, and he almost certainly could not have won re-election in a general election against a Republican or in a Democratic primary against state attorney general Andrew Cuomo, who is likely to defeat former representative Rick Lazio, the apparent Republican nominee.

Race to Watch ***Ohio.*** Gov. Ted Strickland and former U.S. representative John Kasich will be the contestants in one of the nation's most vigorously contested and closely watched races. The *New York Times* wrote in May 2010: "Their contest will speak to one of the biggest questions about the midterm elections: Will voters see enough improvement in the economy—and enough progress from Washington on related issues like health care and curbing the national debt—to grant Democrats more time in power?"[50]

Oklahoma. Gov. Brad Henry is barred by term limits from seeking a third term, and Oklahoma's strong conservative leanings makes it more likely than not that the Republicans will claim the post in the fall. Rep. Mary Fallin and state senator

Randy Brogdon were among the Republicans seeking their party's nomination, and Lt. Gov. Jari Askins and state attorney general Drew Edmondson were running on the Democratic side.

Oregon. Gov. Ted Kulongoski can't seek re-election because of term limits. The May 18 primary election confirmed a November matchup between John Kitzhaber, Kulongoski's two-term predecessor from 1995 through 2002, and Chris Dudley, a businessman known to many Oregonians as a former professional basketball player for the Portland Trailblazers.

Pennsylvania. Gov. Ed Rendell is term-limited, and Dan Onorato, the executive of Allegheny County (Pittsburgh), won a four-candidate Democratic primary in May with 45 percent of the vote. He'll face state attorney general Tom Corbett, who won his primary 69 percent to 31 percent over opponent Sam Rohrer, a state representative.

Tennessee. Democrats will be hard pressed to defend the open governorship in this conservative-leaning state, with outgoing governor Phil Bredesen term-limited. The Democratic nominee will be Mike McWherter, a businessman and the son of a former governor, while the Republicans had a multicandidate primary that included Rep. Zach Wamp, Knoxville mayor Bill Haslam, and Lt. Gov. Ron Ramsey.

Wisconsin. Amid dipping poll numbers, Gov. Jim Doyle announced in August 2009 that he would not seek a third term. The Democratic nominee almost certainly will be Milwaukee mayor Tom Barrett, while Republicans planned to hold a primary that included Milwaukee County executive Scott Walker and former representative Mark Neumann, who narrowly lost a 1998 Senate race to Democratic incumbent Russ Feingold.

Wyoming. Republicans are highly likely to win the governorship in this strongly conservative state because popular governor Dave Freudenthal isn't seeking a third term. (He would have had to overturn a state law limiting governors to only two terms.) The race has drawn seven Republicans and five Democrats.

Republican-Held Seats

Alabama. Gov. Bob Riley can't seek re-election because of term limits. The large Republican field includes former state senator Bradley Byrne and state representative Robert Bentley, who qualified for a July 13 runoff election that will determine the party nominee.

The Democrats nominated state agriculture commissioner Ron Sparks, who defeated Rep. Artur Davis in the Democratic primary by an unexpectedly large margin. Davis was bidding to become the first black governor in Alabama history and only the fifth in U.S. history.

California. Gov. Arnold Schwarzenegger is term-limited. The Republican nominee will be Meg Whitman, the billionaire former chief executive officer of eBay, who defeated state insurance commissioner Steve Poizner in the June primary. Through the end of May, Whitman had spent more than $80 million, including $68 million that she gave her campaign. She has said that she could spend as much as $150 million of her personal fortune on the campaign.[51] Whitman will face Democrat Jerry Brown, the state attorney general, a former two-term governor (1975–1983), and three-time candidate for president.

Connecticut. Popular governor Jodi Rell probably would have won a second term with ease had she chosen to seek it. Republican candidates include Lt. Gov. Michael Fedele and Tom Foley, a former U.S. ambassador to Ireland, while the Democrats will choose between Stamford mayor Dan Malloy and businessman Ned Lamont, who beat Sen. Joseph I. Lieberman in the 2006 Democratic primary but lost in the general election.

Georgia. Former governor Roy Barnes is running to reclaim the office he held from 1999 through 2002, when he was unseated by Republican Sonny Perdue, who is barred by term limits from running again. Several Democrats are challenging Barnes in the primary, and the crowded Republican field includes state insurance commissioner John Oxendine and former representative Nathan Deal.

Hawaii. Given the overall Democratic leanings of President Obama's birth state, Republicans will have to work hard to elect Lt. Gov. Duke Aiona to succeed term-limited governor Linda Lingle. The two major Democratic contenders are former representative Neil Abercrombie and Honolulu mayor Mufi Hanneman.

Minnesota. Gov. Tim Pawlenty could have run for a third term but chose not to, sparking speculation that he has designs on a White House run in 2012. Democratic state House Speaker Margaret Anderson Kelliher received the state party's endorsement at an April 2010 convention, though she will be opposed in the August primary by former U.S. senator Mark Dayton and former state House minority leader Matt Entenza. The Republican nominee will be state representative Tom Emmer.

Rhode Island. This is one of the nation's most strongly Democratic states, and so Republicans will be hard pressed to elect a like-minded successor to term-limited governor Donald Carcieri. Former state representative Victor Moffitt and former Carcieri aide John Robitaille are seeking the Republican nomination, and state attorney general Patrick Lynch and state treasurer Frank Caprio are seeking the Democratic nod.

South Dakota. A large Republican field developed in the race to succeed term-limited governor Mike Rounds. The party nominated lieutenant governor Dennis Daugaard, who is favored to defeat Democratic state senator Scott Heidepriem.

Every midterm election year, prospective candidates in the next presidential election hit the hustings for the party that doesn't hold the White House. Most often these individuals rally in Iowa, New Hampshire, and other early-voting states in the presidential sweepstakes. Among the Republicans weighing a challenge to President Obama are former Alaska governor Sarah Palin, former Massachusetts governor Mitt Romney, and outgoing Minnesota governor Tim Pawlenty, all shown here speaking at campaign-style events in 2010.

Vermont. One of two states to elect its governors to two-year terms (New Hampshire is the other), Vermont will elect a new chief executive to succeed Gov. Jim Douglas, who declined to seek a fifth term. It's looking like Lt. Gov. Brian Dubie will be the Republican nominee opposite the winner of a crowded Democratic primary. Vermont leans Democratic, so this will be a tough governorship for the Republicans to hold.

Dress Rehearsal for 2012

The 2010 midterm elections also will set the stage for the 2012 presidential election, in which President Obama will be seeking re-election against the winner of what should be a multicandidate Republican contest. Because the first primaries and caucuses will occur in January 2012, prospective candidates for the presidency will be announcing their candidacies right after the midterms and laying the groundwork for White House bids well before then. The 2010 midterm elections will give Republican White House hopefuls an opportunity to campaign in key swing states and meet the donors and activists who will be influential in the GOP campaign to defeat President Obama.

Several would-be presidential candidates hit the hustings in 2010. Among them was former Alaska governor Sarah Palin, the 2008 Republican vice-presidential nominee, who visited twenty-four states in late 2009 to promote a new book, *Going Rogue*. She also campaigned for preferred candidates, often announcing endorsements on her Facebook page.

Yet Palin's endorsed candidates had an uneven record of success. A late May campaign visit to assist Republican Vaughn Ward in her native Idaho didn't save him from an embarrassing loss in a primary election. And she endorsed a Mississippi candidate who won just 14 percent of the vote in a June primary.

In early 2009 Palin organized a political action committee, SarahPAC, that will raise money to help fund favored candidates. In the first three months of 2010 Palin's PAC raised $400,000 and spent $402,000, of which just $9,500 went to federal candidates and committees. The PAC had $926,000 left to spend at the beginning of April 2010.[52]

Former Massachusetts governor Mitt Romney, who ran for president in 2008, was gearing up in 2010 to pursue a second White House campaign. He published a book, *No Apology: The Case for American Greatness*, but he kept a lower profile than Palin. He did announce endorsements of and political contributions to preferred candidates through his political committee, Free and Strong America PAC.

In June 2010 Romney campaigned for the re-election of Arizona Republican senator John McCain, a rival for the 2008 Republican presidential nomination. Despite their contentious battle for the White House and obvious disagreements on some issues, Romney appeared in Arizona to ask voters for "a favor. And that's to re-elect the great, strong senator from Arizona, Sen. John McCain."[53]

Another potential Republican White House contender, Minnesota governor Tim Pawlenty, also participated in the 2010 elections. He formed a PAC in October 2009, Freedom First PAC, and appeared in Washington, D.C., later that month to meet with several hundred Republican activists and Capitol Hill aides.[54]

Pawlenty endorsed a host of Republican candidates in competitive races and in June 2010 held a Facebook "town hall" meeting with Sean Duffy, a Wisconsin prosecutor who is seeking the seat of retiring Democratic representative David R. Obey.

Palin, Romney, Pawlenty and some other prominent Republicans weighing 2012 presidential campaigns will all be looking to make a good impression on GOP voters and activists who share their goal of unseating President Obama, who will himself be a visible presence in the 2010 midterm elections as he positions himself to win a second term in 2012.

Dress Rehearsal for 2012 **45**

Notes

1. Thomas M. Davis III, "7 Lessons for Democrats and Republicans from the 2009 Elections," *U.S. News and World Report,* November 6, 2009.
2. Jeffrey M. Jones, "Both Parties' Favorable Ratings Near Record Lows," Gallup, June 1, 2010. Available at www.gallup.com/poll/138095/Parties-Favorable-Ratings-Near-Record-Lows.aspx.
3. Andrew E. Busch, "1946 Midterm Gives GOP First Majority Since 1928 Elections, Helps Ensure Truman's Reelection," Editorial for Ashbrook Center for Public Affairs, June 2006.
4. "1953–1955: The Eighty-Third Congress." CQ Press Electronic Library, *Guide to U.S. Elections* Online Edition, gus6e1–1163–54369–2198587. Originally published in *Guide to U.S. Elections,* 6th ed., vol. 1 (Washington, D.C.: CQ Press, 2010).
5. "1962 Elections—Mixed Pattern of Results," *Congressional Quarterly Weekly Report,* November 9, 1962, 2128.
6. "1969–1971: The Ninety-First Congress." CQ Press Electronic Library, *Guide to U.S. Elections* Online Edition, gus6e1–1163–54369–2198618. Originally published in *Guide to U.S. Elections,* 6th ed., vol. 1 (Washington, D.C.: CQ Press, 2010).
7. "1989–1991: The 101st Congress." CQ Press Electronic Library, *Guide to U.S. Elections* Online Edition, gus6e1–1163–54369–2198655. Originally published in *Guide to U.S. Elections,* 6th ed., vol. 1 (Washington, D.C.: CQ Press, 2010).
8. Ibid.
9. Michael Steele on Fox News, November 4, 2009.
10. Tim Kaine on MSNBC, November 2, 2009.
11. Eric Cantor on Fox News, November 4, 2009.
12. Author's calculation of 2008 presidential vote by state. Available at www.cqpolitics.com/cq-assets/eap/campaigns/girouxgems/2008PresidentialVoteByState.pdf.
13. Jennifer Nasour interviewed on PBS, January 20, 2010.
14. David Axelrod on MSNBC, January 20, 2010.
15. Greg Giroux, "Van Hollen Prepared for Chairmanship of DCCC," *CQ Today,* December 21, 2006.
16. Ibid.
17. Kathleen Hunter, "Menendez Holds His Own at the Helm of Senate Democrats' Fundraising Efforts," *CQ Today,* April 28, 2009.
18. Herb Jackson, "Rough and tumble suits him just fine; Fighting style has marked senator's career," *The Record* (Bergen County, N.J.), November 2, 2006.
19. "GOP chairman Steele backs off Limbaugh criticism," CNN.com, March 3, 2009.
20. Jonathan Martin and Andy Barr, "Michael Steele's very bad week," *Politico,* April 2, 2010.
21. Edward Epstein, "Pelosi: Still GOP's Demon of Choice," *CQ Weekly,* May 31, 2010, page 1318.
22. John McArdle, "NRCC Expands Candidate Management System," *Roll Call,* February 8, 2010.
23. Greg Giroux, "Colorado: Gardner Upped To 'Young Gun'" CQPolitics.com, May 24, 2010. Available at http://blogs.cqpolitics.com/eyeon2010/2010/05/colorado-gardner-upped-to-youn.html.
24. Greg Giroux, "Democrats' New Theme: Results vs. Obstructionism," CQPolitics.com, April 28, 2010. Available at http://blogs.cqpolitics.com/eyeon2010/2010/04/kaine-details-democrats-midter.html.

25. Dan Eggen, "U.S. Chamber of Commerce sets sights on Democrats ahead of midterm elections," *Washington Post*, March 16, 2010.
26. Thomas Donohue, remarks to the National Press Club, May 14, 2010.
27. Dan Eggen, "Interest groups prepared to spend record amounts in 2010 elections," *Washington Post*, June 3, 2010.
28. Peter H. Stone, "Gillespie Raising Funds for New 527," *National Journal* "Under the Influence" blog, March 17, 2010.
29. Joseph J. Schatz, "Reading the Tea Leaves at the Capitol," *CQ Weekly*, March 1, 2010.
30. Alex Knott, "Supreme Court Knocks Down Corporate Spending Limits," CQPolitics.com, January 21, 2010.
31. Thomas Donohue, remarks to National Press Club, May 14, 2010.
32. Obama remarks at Democratic National Committee–Boxer fund-raiser, May 25, 2010.
33. Eric Cantor's Republican response to President Obama's weekly radio address, April 17, 2010.
34. Charlene Carter, "Trimmed-Down Jobs Bill Signed Into Law," *CQ Weekly*, March 22, 2010, page 696.
35. Pelosi interviewed on Bloomberg, May 28, 2010.
36. Alex Wayne and Rebecca Adams, "House Clears Final Health Care Bill," *CQ Today*, March 25, 2010.
37. Obama remarks on health care in Iowa City, Iowa, March 25, 2010.
38. ABC News/*Washington Post* poll conducted June 3–6, 2010. Results available at http://abcnews.go.com/images/PollingUnit/1110a1%20Oil%20Spill.pdf.
39. Donald Lambro, "2010 shaping up badly for Senate Republicans," *Washington Times*, January 18, 2009.
40. Emily Pierce, "Reid: 'They All Scare Me'" *CQ–Roll Call*, May 31, 2010.
41. Democrat Sam Ervin was the last senator to win re-election to this seat. His successors were Democrat Robert Morgan (1975–1981), Republican John East (1981–1986), Republican James Broyhill (1986), Democrat Terry Sanford (1986–1993), Republican Lauch Faircloth (1993–1999), and Democrat John Edwards (1999–2005).
42. Greg Giroux, "McCain: Maverick No More?" *CQ Today*, August 19, 2009.
43. David Margolick, "The McCain Mutiny," *Newsweek*, April 3, 2010. Available at www.newsweek.com/id/235883.
44. "McCain's ultimate maverick move, denial," Politifact.com, April 6, 2010. Available at www.politifact.com/truth-o-meter/statements/2010/apr/06/john-mccain/mccains-ultimate-maverick-move-denial.
45. "House GOP Plans New 'Contract With America' After Labor Day," *Wall Street Journal*, April 20, 2010.
46. Matthew Murray, "Chamber Chief Doesn't Expect Republican House Takeover," CQPolitics.com, May 28, 2010.
47. For a list of these "McCain Democrats," please see Greg's List on CQPolitics.com. Available at www.cqpolitics.com/gregslist.
48. For ratings of all races by CQ and Roll Call, please consult www.cqpolitics.com.
49. Jennifer Steinhauer, "4 Ex-Governors, Older, Grayer and Yearning for Jobs of Yore," *New York Times*, December 6, 2009.
50. Jeff Zeleny, "In Ohio, Gauge for Midterms, Economy Rules," *New York Times*, May 29, 2010.

51. Jack Chang, "Meg Whitman surpasses $80 million in spending on California governor's race," *Sacramento Bee,* May 28, 2010. Available at www.sacbee.com/2010/05/28/2783212/meg-whitman-surpasses-80-million.html.
52. Author's analysis of Sarah PAC's FEC reports, www.fec.gov.
53. Dan Nowicki, "John Shadegg gets 'Jenny's Law' into defense bill," *Arizona Republic,* June 6, 2010.
54. Jonathan Martin, "2012 peek at Pawlenty's PAC fundraiser," *Politico,* October 22, 2009.